What's for dinner?

For the children my children may one day cook for.

What's for dinner?

Easy & delicious recipes for everyday cooking

Fay Ripley

Collins

Contents

HOP SIDES IN

MONDAY TU

ESDSDAY TH

DAY WEEKE

INTRODUCTION

WHAT'S FOR DINNER?

There are only a few things in my life that make me properly happy. It has to be said that a new handbag can lift my spirits for a week or so, as can a session on my teeth whitening home kit. Obviously my children bring the usual surges of love that, in between nit combing and turning nagging into an Olympic sport, provide me with that warm glow of wellbeing. Not to mention a loving husband who appears not to have noticed that his wife has stopped wearing sexy undies and now wears a pinny. All this and the odd walk on a fresh autumn morning can indeed take the credit for some of my happiness. However, the glue that sticks it all together, that turns a moment spent smiling into a memory for life is...*food*.

Food makes us happy. It brings people together for celebrations, comfort, reunions, new beginnings and happy endings. I have marked all my big moments with a cake; from the loss of my first tooth to the crashing of my first car. When I left home at 17, a warming stew was the dish I comforted myself with and a passion fruit pavlova is how I wowed my husband. From the moment we wake up, there is the chance to treat ourselves to many delicious mouthfuls that mean each and every day has its brilliant bits.

Now that I have realised the true potential of each meal, I get 'table rage'. It's like road rage, but not because an old bloke has just cut me up but because a young bloke has just served me a half-frozen chicken Kiev. A wasted meal is a wasted memory and that turns food into fuel, making it just fodder to fill a gap.

Look, I know very well how easy it is to get into a food rut. As a multi-tasking working mum, I slipped into a pattern of feeding the family because I had to. There was no joy left. I'd lost the love, and more to the point I no longer enjoyed making meals or eating them. I was held back so often by recipes that were too long, too complicated and too full of ingredients I'd never used and had no idea where to buy. In essence, my confidence was zapped by exotic spices and rare vegetables.

In this cookbook I'm passing on 100 no-fuss recipes from my kitchen to yours that make it easy to cook tasty, simple food that everyone will enjoy – you included. I've stuck to ingredients you can actually buy and store cupboard dishes you will use time and time again. At home I try and do a bit of the slicing, marinating, grating etc. beforehand so that when I rush in from work or play I can whip up a delicious meal in minutes. Follow the time tips for short cuts and quick cheats. Feel free to chop and change ingredients depending on how fussy your family and friends are. Lists are good, they work. Live off the left-overs.

Try my house rule: if you've cooked for people then the people do the washing up, and if it was top-notch tucker then that makes you a super hero. I have organised the recipes into days of the week, but of course they will all work any day you fancy.

The Cornershop chapter includes dishes that I have knocked up over the last few years using my local store, 'George's'. George, whose real name is Niko, is Turkish and stocks a pretty varied range of groceries, but as not everyone has a George/Niko on the corner, I've kept it simple. Hopefully you can pick up the bits and pieces you need on your own street without too much stress. In fact, stress, or 'food stress', is the very thing I'd like my cookbook to eliminate from your day.

A big part of my motivation when I'm cooking up a storm is showing off. So look out for my easy roasts that will double up for lunch and dinner parties, there are lots of recipes that look posher than they really are and never underestimate how good you will feel when their plates are clean and you haven't even broken into a sweat.

I hope this book will give the timid cook confidence and the confident cook a quick solution. I have been bubbling and boiling away for over two years to bring you recipes that my whole family, from the shortest to the tallest, has given the thumbs up to. I want this book to surprise you, because you are going to surprise yourself. Let's get back in the kitchen, around the table and make some memories so you can get excited again when you hear a little voice in your head ask that daily question, 'What's for Dinner?'.

MONDAY TUESDAY WEDNESDAY THURSDAY

NERSHOP SII
TUESDAY W
HURSDAY FI
END CORNE

MONDAY

Perfect Pea & Bacon Soup

For 4–6
Prep time
10 minutes
Cook time
20 minutes
Freezable
(soup only)

Life brings many surprises. Some of my most memorable include a clapped-out Citroën 2CV wrapped in a big red ribbon on my 21st birthday, meeting my daughter for the first time (I was sure she was a fella) and the slow realisation that I'm never going to fit back into my wedding dress. But there has been nothing more surprising to me than how much my kids love this healthy, creamy, delicious green soup...who knew?

All You Need Is...

1 onion, peeled and chopped
180g smoked streaky
  bacon, chopped
1 tbsp olive oil
1 garlic clove, peeled
  and crushed
1 litre vegetable stock

1kg frozen petits pois
30g fresh mint leaves

Crunchy Croûtons
1 French stick
3 tbsp olive oil

All You Do Is...

1 Preheat the oven to 160°C (fan), 180°C, gas mark 4. In a large heavy-based saucepan fry the onion and bacon in the oil, then when they are cooked through chuck in the garlic and fry for 1 minute.

2 Now pour in your stock and petits pois. Bring to the boil, then cover, turn down the heat and simmer for 15–20 minutes.

3 Meanwhile, tear the loaf into bite-sized pieces, then chuck in a bowl and pour over the olive oil. Get your hands in and really coat the bread. Throw the chunks into a roasting tin and bake for 15 minutes till golden.

4 Whizz two-thirds of the soup mixture in a blender with the mint. Do this in two batches to prevent a pea tsunami. Sieve it back into the pan, working it hard with a wooden spoon to get all that liquid out, then discard the pulp. Voilà!

5 Season with pepper and serve hot with your crunchy croûtons.

Time tip
Make the soup in advance, and reheat when needed.

Baby biz
Make a batch without the bacon when they are very wee.

Cheesy Peasy Omelette

Do try this at home; it's a simple but delicious take on a classic omelette. The freshness of the mint with the smoky flavour from the cheese is a match made in heaven – a five-minute favourite.

For 1
Prep time
5 minutes
Cook time
5 minutes

All You Need Is...

30g frozen petits pois or peas
drizzle of olive oil
2 medium free-range
  eggs, beaten
50g hard smoked
  cheese, grated

sprinkle of chopped
  fresh mint
sprinkle of grated
  Parmesan cheese

All You Do Is...

1 Pour boiling water over the peas to cover and leave to stand for 5 minutes, then drain.

2 Heat a drizzle of oil in a frying pan over a medium heat. Wipe the pan round carefully with some kitchen paper to coat the pan.

3 Pour in the beaten eggs and when it just starts bubbling on the top, after about 2 minutes, sprinkle the smoked cheese down the centre, then the peas and mint. Now sprinkle the Parmesan over the whole omelette, and flip half over to make a half moon, press down gently and cook for 1 more minute. Season and serve with a crisp salad or chips if it's the hols.

Other stuff
Keep the omelette warm in a low oven while you make more.

Ping Pong Chicken Noodle Salad

For 4
Prep time
20 minutes
Cook time
15 minutes

'Ping pong' is my take on 'bang bang'. The nutty sweet sauce with the soft chicken, crunchy veg and glassy noodles give us all a zing zing in the ying yang, which is yum yum in our tum tum.

All You Need Is...

100g cashew nuts
150g runner beans,
   trimmed and stringed
2 carrots, peeled
¼ cucumber
3 spring onions
1 iceberg lettuce
1 x 300g pack fresh
   rice noodles
300–400g leftover cooked
   free-range chicken, shredded

1 tbsp black sesame seeds
   (optional)
Dressing
2 tbsp tahini paste
1 tbsp light soy sauce
1 tbsp sweet chilli sauce
1 tbsp rice vinegar
100ml chicken stock
juice of 1 lime

All You Do Is...

1 Preheat the oven to 180°C (fan), 200°C, gas mark 6. Roast the cashews in the oven for 10 minutes till just golden (don't forget them). Cool then roughly chop and set aside.

2 Blanch the runner beans in a pan of boiling water for 3–4 minutes. Drain and rinse in cold water, then slice them lengthways to make matchsticks. Finely slice the carrots, cucumber and spring onions into strips.

3 Line your bowls with a large outside lettuce leaf or two. Whisk all the dressing ingredients together, then mix half of it with the noodles and chopped veg, and fill each lettuce bowl.

4 Scatter the chicken on top, then drizzle over the rest of the dressing followed by the chopped cashews and a sprinkling of black sesame seeds, if using.

Time tip
Use ready-trimmed runner beans, pre-roast the nuts, make the dressing beforehand and keep in the fridge.

Trout Puff Parcel

Shop-bought puff pastry is a great standby in the fridge and I love the gentle flavours of this fish with the smooth spinach and punchy pesto. A favourite with all ages served with Crunchy Coleslaw (see page 220) and My Big Green Salad (see page 35).

For 4
Prep time
15 minutes
Cook time
30 minutes

All You Need Is...

1 x 250g pack baby spinach
1 x 375g pack ready-rolled
 puff pastry
4 sea trout or salmon fillets
 (about 150g each fish),
 skinned

4 tsp fresh pesto (buy
 or make it, see page 214)
1 unwaxed lemon

All You Do Is...

1 Preheat the oven to 200°C (fan), 220°C, gas mark 7. Line an oven tray with baking paper.

2 Gently cook the spinach in a covered pan for a few minutes until wilted. Cool a little, then press out as much of the water as possible (I use my hands) and roughly chop.

3 Unroll the pastry on the lined tray and cut in half. Put half the spinach on each as a base then put two fish fillets snugly next to each other on top followed by a teaspoon of the pesto spread over each fillet. Grate over some lemon zest and fold up each parcel, pinching the edges shut. Trim off any excess pastry.

4 Bake for 25 minutes. To serve, make two portions by slicing each parcel down the middle to show off those lovely layers.

Time tip
Fine made a few hours in advance and kept in the fridge ready for cooking. If you have time, beat an egg and brush over the top of each parcel before baking.

Baby biz
Just roast a piece of fish beside your pastry parcels and whizz with a little pesto and spinach. Watch out for bones.

Festive Pig in a Bun

For 4
Prep time
10 minutes
Cook time
25 minutes
Freezable
(raw)

This is a great Boxing day special that is now a start-of-the-week favourite with my little piglets. Perfect for picnics or make mini versions for parties – just don't wait till Xmas.

All You Need Is...

8 of your favourite
  British sausages
80g dried cranberries

80g pine nuts
4 fresh, crusty rolls, to serve

All You Do Is...

1 Preheat the oven to 180°C (fan), 200°C, gas mark 6. Line a large baking tray with baking parchment.

2 Skin the sausages and pop the meat in a bowl. Finely chop the cranberries and add them to the sausagemeat with the pine nuts. Get stuck in with damp hands and mix it all together. Take golf-ball-sized scoops and shape into 8 balls then flatten them into patties.

3 Pop the patties onto the baking tray and roast for 25 minutes till golden and crispy. Serve two patties in a fresh crusty roll stuffed with Crunchy Coleslaw (see page 220), and at Xmas a crumbling of Stilton.

Storage stuff
Make extra patties and freeze them raw, then defrost thoroughly before cooking.

Time tip
Make to the end of step 2 and keep in the fridge.

Portobello Road Pasta

I have a love affair with the meaty portobello but other mushrooms work just as well. The tang of mustard with the creamy sauce is the perfect balance and this dish slips down easily as a starter or main. I serve it with a crunchy green salad.

For 2–3
Prep time
5 minutes
Cook time
15 minutes

All You Need Is...

250g dried fettuccine
250g portobello
   mushrooms, thinly sliced
splash of olive oil
few fresh thyme sprigs,
   leaves only

1 fat garlic clove,
   peeled and crushed
150ml chicken or
   vegetable stock
1 tsp Dijon mustard
1 tbsp half-fat crème fraîche

All You Do Is...

1 Cook your pasta following the pack instructions and at the same time, fry the mushrooms in the oil in a frying pan for 7–8 minutes till soft. Throw in the thyme and garlic and fry for another 2 minutes. Grind over a little pepper.

2 Now mix the stock and mustard together, then pour into the pan and allow to bubble for 1 minute. Take off the heat and stir through the crème fraîche.

3 Drain the pasta and toss through the sauce. Season and serve.

Time tip
You can pre-make the sauce but hold back the crème fraîche. Add 2-3 tablespoons of the pasta water to refresh the sauce.

Quick Roll-up Chicken

So simple. The super tasty juices run out when the chicken breasts are sliced and because they are rolled up everyone will think it's really 'restauranty'...expect a big tip and clean plates. Serve with creamy mashed potato and peas.

For 4
Prep time
5 minutes
Cook time
25 minutes

All You Need Is...

4 free-range skinless chicken breasts
4 slices Parma ham

120g garlic and herb soft cheese

All You Do Is...

1 Preheat the oven to 180°C (fan), 200°C, gas mark 6. With a rolling pin, bash out the breasts till they are flatish and twice the size.

2 Lay a slice of ham on each breast and spread a quarter of the soft cheese over it.

3 Roll up the first breast like a Swiss roll then pop in the middle of a piece of foil and wrap it like a Christmas cracker, twisting the ends to seal. Repeat with the other breasts.

4 Put the parcels on a baking tray and bake for 25 minutes. Remove the foil from the chicken, slice on the tray and pour over those yummy juices. Season.

Time tip
Prepare the chicken, wrap in the foil and keep ready in the fridge, then bake as above.

Kids stuff
What's not to like?

Baby biz
Great chopped or whizzed and served with mash.

No-fuss Smoked Salmon & Goat's Cheese Risotto

For 4
Prep time
10 minutes
Cook time
25 minutes

A salmon and creamy cheese combination always hits the spot. I have made sure this cheat's version of cooking the risotto leaves you time to have a cuppa, call a friend, give yourself a foot rub or give someone else a foot rub! High on taste, low on maintenance.

All You Need Is...

1 large onion, peeled
   and finely chopped
1 tbsp olive oil
20g butter
250g risotto rice
800ml chicken stock

finely grated zest of
   1 unwaxed lemon
100g soft goat's cheese
150g smoked salmon,
   roughly chopped into strips
10g fresh dill, chopped

All You Do Is...

1 In a heavy-based pan, fry the onion in the oil and butter till soft, about 5 minutes.

2 Add the rice and stir for a minute or so, then add the stock and lemon zest. Bring to the boil, stir once, then turn the heat down, pop a lid on and simmer for 15 minutes till the rice is cooked but still has a little bite.

3 Now crumble in the goat's cheese and stir till it melts into the creamy rice. Grind in a good amount of black pepper, then stir through the salmon and dill. Season and serve.

One-pan Creamy Spring Chicken Supper

For 4
Prep time
15 minutes
Cook time
25 minutes

I absolutely love one-pot cooking especially if I'm on holiday and don't have all my stuff, or my dishwasher! This is a fabulous combination that you can serve in any season. It's a comforting, delicious, one-pan wonder.

All You Need Is...

4 small free-range skinless
  chicken breasts
  (about 150g each)
splash of olive oil
1 fat garlic clove, peeled
  and crushed
400g new potatoes, skin on
  and very thinly sliced

500ml chicken stock
200g frozen peas
200g broccoli florets,
  cut in half
2 tsp Dijon mustard
2 tbsp natural goat's yoghurt
  or natural yoghurt
80g soft goat's cheese

All You Do Is...

1 In a large, deep non-stick frying pan, fry the chicken in the oil for 5 minutes on each side till golden.

2 Throw in the garlic and fry for 1 minute till just golden, then chuck in the potatoes and stock. Cover and simmer for another 10 minutes.

3 Chuck in the green veg, pop the lid back on and cook for 5 more minutes. Make sure the chicken is cooked through as it depends on the size of the breasts.

4 Stir in the Dijon and yoghurt, then crumble over the goat's cheese. Season and serve.

Baby biz
Finely chop or whizz a bit of everything.

My Big Green Salad

I always have a big green salad on the table. The kids prefer their veg with a little dressing on and, like a lucky dip, will usually find something in there that meets their approval. Feel free to add or take away as you like, and use any seasonal goodies you can get your hands on.

For 4–6
Prep time
10 minutes
Cook time
5 minutes

All You Need Is...

200g runner beans, trimmed,
   stringed and sliced
350g frozen petits pois
1 courgette, trimmed
1 x 200g bag baby spinach
30g fresh mint leaves, chopped

Dressing
3 tbsp olive oil
1 tbsp white wine vinegar
1 tsp Dijon mustard

All You Do Is...

1 Throw the runner beans in a pan of boiling water and simmer for 4–5 minutes, throwing in the petits pois a minute before the beans are ready. Drain and rinse under cold running water.

2 Using a potato peeler, slice very thin strips of courgette lengthways. Mix all the dressing ingredients together with a fork.

3 Throw everything into a large serving bowl and toss together. Season and serve with anything, frankly.

Best-ever Chocolate Banana Bread

For 8
(or just you)

Prep time
20 minutes

Cook time
60 minutes

Freezable

After ten years of marriage, I finally gave in to my husband's whingeing to bake his favourite thing in the world – banana bread. But I don't like banana bread (she stamps her foot), so I added chocolate and I love it. Now I'm happy to bake it and he is allowed a small slice...which is nice of me.

All You Need Is...

130g butter, softened
150g light brown soft sugar
3 ripe bananas (about 300g),
   peeled and mashed
1 tsp vanilla extract
2 large free-range eggs

250g plain flour
1 tsp baking powder
1 tsp bicarbonate of soda
150g dark chocolate,
   broken into chunks
3 tbsp milk

All You Do Is...

1 Preheat the oven to 160°C (fan), 180°C, gas mark 4. Butter or line the loaf tin with baking parchment.

2 Cream the butter and sugar together in a large bowl till fluffy. Add the mashed bananas, vanilla and eggs and whisk together.

3 Sift in the flour, baking powder and bicarbonate of soda and mix in well. Fold in the chocolate chunks and milk till combined.

4 Plop the lot into the lined tin and bake for 50-60 minutes, till risen and golden and a skewer inserted into the bread comes out clean. Cool slightly in the tin, then serve warm if possible for total joy.

Storage stuff
Stored in an airtight container, this cake keeps well for a couple of days.

Other stuff
Use up all those ropey old bananas.

Rise & Shine
Recession Granola

I live off this. It's healthy, won't break the bank and is well worth the effort. A batch will see our family through the whole week. Try it with yoghurt and fruit. And because a thin lady in a gym told me once, 'cereal for dinner is good for weight loss', sometimes I'll have a bowl for my tea. Problem is I have dinner as well.

For 4
Prep time
5 minutes
Cook time
30 minutes

All You Need Is...

400g jumbo oats
100g mixed seeds
   (sunflower, pumpkin and
   sesame seeds work well)

50g walnuts, broken up
2 tbsp runny honey
2 tbsp vegetable oil
150g currants

All You Do Is...

1 Preheat the oven to 180°C (fan), 200°C, gas mark 6. In a large bowl, mix the oats, seeds and walnuts together.

2 Thoroughly work in the honey and oil, then spread out over a large baking tray and bake for 15 minutes. Stir again then put back in for another 5 minutes. A last stir and back in for 5 minutes. It should be golden but not burnt, so bake for an extra 5 minutes if needed.

3 Mix in the currants as soon as you take it out of the oven, then leave to cool completely.

Storage stuff
This keeps for weeks in an airtight container.

Kids stuff
They also love it dry as a snack or sprinkled over ice-cream.

SIDES MONDA
WEDNESDAY
FRIDAY WEE
ERSHOP SID

TUESDAY

Our Favourite
Fast Fishcakes

Makes
8 cakes to
serve 4

Prep time
15 minutes
(plus chilling)

Cook time
30 minutes

Freezable
(raw)

Fishcakes can be a little bland, but the smoky trout and crispy polenta coating give these zing and attitude. Quick, easy and terribly tasty.

All You Need Is...

300g potatoes
  peeled and chopped
300g cooked smoked trout
  (approx. 4 fillets)
finely grated zest and juice
  of 1 unwaxed lemon
1 tsp Dijon mustard

handful of fresh chives
2 big tbsp dried polenta
good glug of olive oil

Sauce
4 tbsp half-fat crème fraîche
1 tsp Dijon mustard

All You Do Is...

1 Boil the spuds until cooked, then drain, mash and leave to cool.

2 Flake the fish into a bowl, then add the lemon zest and juice, Dijon, a grind of pepper and snip in the chives.

3 Throw in the mash and mix really well. Take tablespoons of the mixture and form into 8 patties, then toss each one gently in the polenta. Keep covered in the fridge for at least 30 minutes.

4 Heat the oil in a non-stick pan and fry the fishcakes gently till golden, about 3 minutes on each side.

5 For the sauce, mix the crème fraîche and Dijon together. Season and serve the fishcakes with the mustardy sauce on the side.

Time tip
A great one to pre-prepare and pop in the fridge.

Baby biz
Check for bones. No need to form into cakes and fry, just warm the mixture through thoroughly before serving.

Hot Pesto Chicken Nuggets

For 2–3
Prep time
5 minutes
Cook time
20 minutes
Freezable
(cooked only)

A quick crunchy tea that's bursting with flavour, these nuggets are great cold for picnics and lunchboxes or as a summer lunch when you want to spend less time in the kitchen and more time in the garden.

All You Need Is...

2 plump free-range skinless chicken breasts
2 tbsp red pesto

1 tsp harissa paste
4 tbsp couscous

All You Do Is...

1 Preheat the oven to 180°C (fan), 200°C, gas mark 6. Slice the chicken into goujons (bite-sized pieces).

2 Mix the pesto and harissa really well with the chicken pieces until thoroughly coated, then add the uncooked couscous and toss through to coat again.

3 Spread the chicken pieces out on a non-stick roasting tray and bake for 20 minutes till the chicken is crispy and cooked through. Serve with Crunchy Coleslaw (see page 220) or some potato wedges.

Kids stuff
Adjust the harissa if they DON'T like it hot.

Grown-up stuff
Adjust the harissa if you DO like it hot.

Roast Garlic & Thyme Mushrooms

I've given this classic combination of mushrooms with garlic and thyme a tangy nutty crust, which means you can serve this dish as a starter, side or main.

For 4

Prep time
10 minutes

Cook time
30 minutes

All You Need Is...

4 large portobello mushrooms
40g butter
1 tbsp fresh thyme leaves
1 tbsp olive oil
finely grated zest of
   1 unwaxed lemon

2 garlic cloves, peeled
   and crushed
1 tsp Dijon mustard
4 heaped tsp ground almonds

All You Do Is...

1 Preheat the oven to 180°C (fan), 200°C, gas mark 6. Pop the mushrooms in an ovenproof dish, cut the butter into little knobs, and scatter on top.

2 In a bowl, mix together the thyme leaves, oil, lemon zest, garlic and Dijon. Spoon on top of the mushrooms then sprinkle over the almonds.

3 Roast for 25-30 minutes, or till the topping is golden. Season and serve with a rocket salad on a piece of garlic bread or on their tod as a side dish.

Roasted Tomato & Prosciutto Penne

For 4

Prep time
10 minutes

Cook time
45 minutes

Freezable
(sauce only)

The sweet roasted garlic and tomatoes give this a taste of sunsets that takes me back to warm, lazy days in Italy with my then boyfriend as I waited patiently for a proposal. Well, eventually I prized one out of him and the memories are still as sweet as the dish.

All You Need Is...

500g tomatoes
4 large garlic cloves,
   unpeeled
2 tbsp olive oil

6 slices (90g) prosciutto
10g fresh basil leaves
300g dried penne

All You Do Is...

1 Preheat the oven to 180°C (fan), 200°C, gas mark 6. Take out and discard the green core from the tomatoes and slice in half horizontally. Place them on an oven tray with the garlic and drizzle over the oil. Roast for 30 minutes.

2 Now lay the prosciutto on top of the tomatoes and roast for a further 15 minutes. Remove the prosciutto and set aside.

3 Squeeze out the sweet roasted garlic flesh into a food processor and roughly whizz with the basil and tomatoes.

4 Cook the penne following the pack instructions, then drain. Using your hands, crush over the crispy prosciutto and toss through with your tomato sauce. Serve with a picture postcard of an Italian sunset in front of you.

Quick-rub Lamb Chops

Rubbing oil and a couple of strong flavours into meat or fish lets you whip up a tasty feast in just minutes. Buy the chops on your way home from work and keep some ground spices in the cupboard, then Bob's your uncle...well, John's my uncle, but a quick rub is definitely the way to fabulous fast food.

For 4
Prep time
5 minutes
(plus marinating)

Cook time
20 minutes

Freezable
(raw, marinated lamb only)

All You Need Is...

1 tbsp olive oil
2 tsp ground cumin
2 tsp ground ginger
1 tbsp balsamic vinegar
8 lean lamb chops
   (about 100g each)

350g couscous
1 x 200g pot hummus,
   to serve (buy or make
   it, see page 158)

All You Do Is...

1 Mix the oil, cumin, ginger and vinegar together and rub all over the chops. Cover with cling film and pop in the fridge overnight or for at least half an hour.

2 In a non-stick frying pan, cook the chops over a fairly high heat, about 5 minutes on each side. Meanwhile, make the couscous following the pack instructions (or see page 217). Serve the chops on a bed of couscous with a dollop of hummus.

Best Cottage Pie

For 4

Prep time
20 minutes

Cook time
40 minutes

Freezable
(assembled,
uncooked)

A midweek supper that tastes even better heated the next day ticks a lot of boxes for me. This is a very tasty version of an old favourite... I'd be happy if someone said that about me, frankly.

All You Need Is...

500g potatoes
250g parsnips
big knob of butter
1 onion, peeled and
    finely chopped
splash of olive oil
500g lean mince beef

1 beef stock cube
1 x 400g tin chopped
    tomatoes
2 tbsp tomato purée
1 tbsp Worcestershire sauce
2 tbsp tomato ketchup

All You Do Is...

1 Peel and chop the potatoes and parsnips. Boil until soft, then drain and mash with the butter till smooth. Set aside.

2 Preheat the oven to 180°C (fan), 200°C, gas mark 6. Fry the onion in the oil for 5 minutes or so, then add the mince and fry, turning, till it browns. Dissolve the stock cube with 3 tablespoons of boiling water, then add to the mince along with the rest of the ingredients and mix together.

3 Scrape it all into an ovenproof dish and top with rough dollops of the mash. Bake for 30 minutes till the topping starts to brown. Serve when cooled a little.

Time tip
Great to make and assemble up to a day before, then bake when you need it.

Quick Garlic & Sesame Lime Pork

For 4
Prep time
5 minutes
Cook time
10 minutes

Pork loin is perfect for a speedy supper. It takes only minutes to cook and these fresh flavours give it a strong Aussie accent. Make this and make it a 'G'day'.

All You Need Is...

1 tbsp olive oil
knob of butter
1 tbsp sesame seeds
finely grated zest and juice
    of 2 large limes
400g pork tenderloin, sliced
    into strips
3 garlic cloves,
    peeled and crushed

½ fresh red chilli, deseeded
handful of fresh coriander,
    roughly chopped
2 x 300g packs fresh egg
    noodles
splash of toasted sesame oil

All You Do Is...

1 Heat the olive oil and butter in a frying pan or wok till just sizzling. Throw in the sesame seeds, lime zest, the pork and lastly the crushed garlic and stir gently for 8–10 minutes till the pork is cooked through.

2 Take off the heat, finely chop in a little chilli to taste then dress it with the lime juice and coriander.

3 Meanwhile, thoroughly heat through the noodles in a frying pan or wok then dress with the sesame oil. Season and serve the lime pork tumbling over the noodles.

Kids stuff
Mine love this with the coriander and chilli taken out; I love it as it is.

Italian Crispy Stuffed Chicken

Easy to prepare and even easier to eat. Cooking is sometimes just about combining your favourite flavours and then sitting back to enjoy your family eating them together.

For 4

Prep time
10 minutes

Cook time
30 minutes

Freezable
(raw. Cook from frozen and increase cook time by 15-20 minutes)

All You Need Is...

8 free-range chicken thighs, boned and skinned
8 tsp fresh pesto (buy or make it, see page 214)
100g mozzarella cheese

100g fresh breadcrumbs
2 tbsp olive oil

Equipment
8 cocktail sticks

All You Do Is...

1 Preheat the oven to 180°C (fan), 200°C, gas mark 0.

2 Unroll and lay the chicken thighs flat. Pop a small teaspoon of pesto and a knob of mozzarella in the middle and roll up again securing with a cocktail stick. Lay them snugly side by side in an ovenproof dish or on a baking tray, with the joins tucked underneath.

3 Toss the breadcrumbs in the oil and use to cover the thighs. Pop in the oven for 30 minutes till the chicken is cooked through and the topping is crispy. Season and serve with Little Italian Roasties (see page 216) or your favourite roast veg.

All-in-one Paella

For 4
Prep time
15 minutes
Cook time
20 minutes

Paella can be a challenge for younger kids but this one is wolfed down by everybody, with its sweet smoky flavours wafting through the house. It's a great 'one-dish wonder' for friends and family.

All You Need Is...

1 onion, peeled and chopped
1 red pepper, sliced
75g chorizo, chunky slices
1 tbsp olive oil
2 garlic cloves,
   peeled and crushed
½ tsp sweet smoked paprika
200g runner beans, trimmed,
   stringed and sliced

250g white basmati rice,
   rinsed
1 x 400g tin chopped
   tomatoes
500ml chicken stock
grated zest of 1 unwaxed
   lemon
200g peeled raw tiger prawns

All You Do Is...

1 In a shallow casserole dish or frying pan with a lid, fry the onion, pepper and chorizo in the oil for 5 minutes, then add the garlic and paprika and fry for 1 more minute.

2 Now add the beans and rice. Give it a good stir and pop in the tomatoes, stock and lemon zest.

3 Cover and cook over a high heat for 10 minutes.

4 Bung the prawns on top, cover and cook for a couple of minutes till they are cooked through and the rice is tender. Season and serve in one big dish in the middle of the table.

Time tip
Pre-chop, then whip it up in minutes, when you are ready. Use ready-prepared runner beans.

Kids stuff
If prawns are a challenge use small pieces of free-range chicken or pork loin, which work brilliantly fried with the onion.

Crispy Soy Mackerel

This is without doubt my favourite fish in the very clever sea. Cook it in any which way you please; its creamy flesh and gentle flavours will delight the whole family. The fiddly bit of pulling out the bones can be done in advance, then it takes just minutes to prepare. If you are really up against it, you can use scissors and cut the bony spine out completely, leaving you with the goujons.

For 4

Prep time
15 minutes
(plus chilling, optional)

Cook time
20 minutes

All You Need Is...

2 unwaxed lemons
1 x 2cm piece fresh ginger, peeled
4 large tbsp fresh breadcrumbs
2 tbsp sesame seeds

2 tbsp olive oil
4 large mackerel fillets (about 150–175g each), skin on and boned
1 tbsp light soy sauce

All You Do Is...

1 Preheat the oven to 180°C (fan), 200°C, gas mark 6. For the topping, finely zest the lemons and grate the ginger into the breadcrumbs, then mix with the sesame seeds and oil.

2 Put your prepared mackerel in an ovenproof dish and spoon over the soy sauce and juice from the lemons. (Leaving it in the fridge for half an hour is a bonus).

3 Scatter the crumb mix on top of the fish and bake for 20 minutes till the fish flakes and the topping is golden. Serve with some crispy stir-fried vegetables.

Time tip
Always have breadcrumbs in the freezer – never waste a stale end of loaf.

Other stuff
Feel with your fingers for any bones, I use my eyebrow tweezers to remove them (washed in the dishwasher).

Kids stuff
Save on extra maths tuition and feed them more of this tasty brain food.

Baby biz
For very little ones just leave out the soy.

Baby Toads in Baby Holes

For 6

Prep time
10 minutes

Cook time
30–35 minutes

Sausages are a staple at the Ripley kitchen table and these make a really tasty change. Baby toads go very well down grown-up holes too.

All You Need Is...

120g plain flour
2 large free-range eggs
350ml milk
10–15 large fresh sage
   leaves, chopped

2 tbsp olive oil
12 British chipolatas

Equipment
12-hole muffin tray

All You Do Is...

1 Preheat the oven to 220°C (fan), 240°C, gas mark 9. Using an electric whisk, beat the flour and eggs together in a large bowl, then gradually add the milk to form a batter. Add the sage.

2 Oil the muffin tray using a little of the olive oil. Add a teaspoon of the oil to every hole and bend 1 chipolata into each hole. Bake for 15 minutes then ladle the batter evenly into all the holes.

3 Lower the oven temperature to 200°C (fan), 220°C, gas mark 7 and cook for a further 15–20 minutes, or till golden and crispy. Serve with ketchup and French beans (frogs legs!).

Time tip
Make the batter beforehand if you want to and store in the fridge.

Kids stuff
I tell them the green bits are the toad's skin.

Auntie Aggie

For 6–8
Prep time
15 minutes
(plus chilling)
Cook time
5 minutes

I have absolutely no idea why this white chocolate and rasberry crunch is called Auntie Aggie, but as a child it was always the cake my mum made me for birthdays. It's a quick, easy dessert with none of the bother of cheesecake but all of the pleasure. Mum still makes it and I still absolutely love it. Thanks Auntie Aggie, whoever you are...

All You Need Is...

100g butter
300g plain chocolate
   digestives, crushed
   into crumbs
225ml double cream
1 vanilla pod, halved
   lengthways
225ml half-fat crème fraîche

150g white chocolate,
   finely grated
250g fresh raspberries
a little grated dark chocolate,
   to decorate

Equipment
24cm springform cake tin

All You Do Is...

1 Line the cake tin with baking parchment.

2 Melt the butter gently in a pan then add the biscuit crumbs and mix well. Using the back of a spoon, press the crumb mix down into the tin to form a base, then pop it in the fridge for 15 minutes.

3 Just before serving, whip the double cream till it just starts to thicken, scrape in the vanilla seeds from your pod and whip in the crème fraîche. Fold in the white chocolate then gently turn in most of the raspberries. Pile on top of the base. Decorate with a grating of dark chocolate and the remaining raspberries, then ease out of the tin, remove the paper and stand back to avoid the stampede.

Time tip
You can make the base well in advance and pre-grate the chocolate.

Other stuff
Whip through a tablespoon of Baileys or Kahlua for dinner parties...or when the vicar is round.

Quick Chocolate Pear Crumbles

For 4

Prep time
5 minutes

Cook time
20 minutes

I never intend to buy chocolate digestives; they just end up in my trolley by magic. Then they end up in my mouth without so much as an invitation. It normally happens mid-morning when I'm at my most vulnerable to snacks. Pledges of 'I'll stick to dried fruit next time' calm my thoughts, along with the brilliant plan of crumbling a few from the bottom of the ravaged digestives packet over some juicy fresh pears for everyone's tea. Once again proving to myself that I was just thinking of others, and I simply must have bought those biccies to make the family happy.

All You Need Is...

20g blanched hazelnuts
3 dark chocolate digestives
2 big ripe pears

30g dark chocolate
(at least 70% cocoa solids),
roughly broken up

All You Do Is...

1 Preheat the oven to 180°C (fan), 200°C, gas mark 6.

2 In a plastic food bag, bash the nuts and biscuits to break them up into rough crumbs.

3 Cut the pears in half and scoop out the core with a teaspoon. Place the pears in a small ovenproof dish and fill with the crumbs then push in the chocolate bits.

4 Bake for 20 minutes till the chocolate is melting and the pears are warm and juicy. Serve with a ball of vanilla ice cream on top.

AY TUESDAY

THURSDAY

ND CORNER

MONDAY TUE

WEDNESDAY

Nutty Mango Rice Salad

For 8
Prep time
20 minutes
Cook time
10 minutes

Fresh and fruity, this bright salad is a celebration on the plate and is great with barbecues or lunch in the park. My girlfriends text me to make sure it's on the menu.

All You Need Is...

250g white basmati rice, cooked (see page 227)
150g cashew nuts
100g frozen petits pois
3 salad onions, trimmed and finely chopped
1 big bunch of fresh mint, chopped
1 bunch of fresh coriander, chopped (optional)

2 mangoes, peeled, stoned and diced
50g desiccated coconut
1 red chilli, deseeded and finely chopped

Dressing
juice of 2 lemons
1 tsp sherry vinegar
2 tbsp olive oil
2 tbsp toasted sesame oil

All You Do Is...

1 Preheat the oven to 180°C (fan), 200°C, gas mark 6. While your rice is cooking and cooling, roast the cashews for 8–10 minutes (don't forget them). Cool and break up into a big bowl.

2 Pour boiling water over the petits pois, cover and leave for 5 minutes. Drain and add to the bowl along with the rest of the salad ingredients and the cold rice.

3 Mix the dressing ingredients and toss everything together, then season and serve.

Storage stuff
It's best eaten on the day it's made.

Kids stuff
The coriander is often a step too far for my kids.

Other stuff
Amazing with fish (see page 128) and chicken.

Mini Cheese & Tomato Frittata

These are fun and very useful. Serve them in their paper jackets piled high for everyone to grab, then hold back a couple for your lunch tomorrow.

Makes
12
Prep time
15 minutes
Cook time
20 minutes

All You Need Is...

6 large free-range eggs
2 courgettes, trimmed
and finely chopped
1 big tbsp fresh chives,
chopped
60g Gruyère cheese,
finely grated

120ml milk
12 cherry tomatoes, halved

Equipment
12-hole muffin tray

All You Do Is...

1 Preheat the oven to 180°C (fan), 200°C, gas make 6. Line the muffin tray with a square (about 15cm) of baking paper roughly pushed into each hole.

2 Lightly beat the eggs then add the courgettes, chives, Gruyère and milk. Season and mix together.

3 Ladle the mix into the holes, pop 2 halved tomatoes on top and bake for 20 minutes till firm and golden on top. Serve warm with a salad and crusty bread or pop in a lunchbox.

Quick Zingy Kebabs
with Tzatziki

For 4
Prep time
20 minutes
Cook time
5 minutes
Freezable
(raw,
marinated
lamb only)

This is holiday food. This is late-night-can't-remember-your-own-name food. It's fun to eat and hits those taste buds running.

All You Need Is...

400g lamb leg steak
1 tsp harissa paste
1 tsp tomato purée
1 tbsp olive oil
3 medium carrots, peeled
  and roughly grated
10g fresh mint leaves,
  chopped

juice of ½ lemon
flatbreads or pitta, to serve

Tzatziki
¼ cucumber
3 tbsp Greek yoghurt
1 garlic clove, peeled
  and crushed
juice of ½ lemon

All You Do Is...

1 Chop the lamb into bite-sized chunks and toss with the harissa, tomato purée and oil.

2 For the salad, mix the carrots, mint and lemon juice together in a bowl.

3 For the tzatziki, deseed and finely chop the cucumber, then mix with the yoghurt, garlic and lemon juice.

4 Preheat a non-stick frying or griddle pan, then tip the lamb and its marinade into the hot pan and fry for 4–5 minutes, turning the meat a couple of times till just cooked. To serve, just pile a little salad, tzatziki and lamb into your flatbreads, season and that's dinner all wrapped up.

Time tip
The harissa-covered lamb can marinate in the fridge overnight if you would like a stronger flavour, and the garnishes can be made in advance.

Kids stuff
Back off the harissa if it's scaring anyone, but this amount works for mine.

Hoisin Pork Fillet with Lemon & Ginger Noodles

For 4
Prep time
10 minutes
Cook time
30 minutes

Who needs a takeaway when you can whip up this tangy Chinese feast in no time. Steam some pak choi or Tenderstem broccoli alongside and feel free to serve with rice if you prefer; a real crowd pleaser.

All You Need Is...

450–500g trimmed
  British pork fillet
3 tbsp Hoisin sauce
200g Tenderstem broccoli
3 spring onions, trimmed
  and sliced
1 x 2.5cm piece fresh ginger,
  peeled and finely grated

2 garlic cloves, peeled
  and crushed
1 tbsp sesame seeds
2 tbsp sesame oil
1 x 400g pack
  fresh egg noodles
juice of 1 lemon

All You Do Is...

1 Preheat the oven 180°C (fan), 200°C, gas mark 6. Place the pork fillet on a piece of foil on a small baking tray and smother it in the Hoisin. Cook in the oven for 30 minutes then take out and leave to rest for 5 minutes.

2 Meanwhile, chuck the broccoli into a pan of boiling water for 3–4 minutes, then drain.

3 In a wok or large frying pan, lightly fry the spring onions, ginger, garlic and sesame seeds in a tablespoon of the oil for just a minute. Add the cooked broccoli and noodles and heat through thoroughly. Dress with another tablespoon of the oil and the lemon juice. Carve the pork into thick slices and serve on top of the noodles in a bowl, with all the juices available.

Baby biz
Roast a piece of the pork without the sauce alongside yours.

Time tip
Peel then freeze your ginger whole. It's so much easier to grate from frozen and stops any waste.

Chicken Tonnata
with Lemon New Potatoes

For 4
Prep time
20 minutes
Cook time
25 minutes

Inspired by the Italian veal dish that I have loved for years, this surprising combo of gentle smooth textures with a zing of lemon and capers works a treat. It's great with asparagus too.

All You Need Is...

3–4 free-range skinless
   chicken breasts
1 carrot, peeled and cut
   in half
½ onion, peeled
1 bay leaf
1 tbsp capers, drained

Tonnata sauce
100g line-caught tinned tuna
3 tbsp good mayo

1 tbsp olive oil
juice of 1 lemon
2 anchovy fillets

Lemon new potatoes
500g baby new potatoes,
   skin on and halved
finely grated zest and
   juice of 1 unwaxed lemon
good glug of olive oil

All You Do Is...

1 To poach the chicken, half fill a large saucepan with water. Drop in the carrot halves, onion and bay leaf and bring to the boil. Pop in the chicken breasts, turn down the heat, pop the lid on and simmer for 20 minutes till the chicken is cooked through and tender.

2 While the chicken is cooking, boil the spuds. After 15-20 minutes, check if they're cooked by sticking a fork in a spud. If it easily falls off your fork then it's good to go. Drain and slice. Toss the potatoes with the lemon juice, zest and oil, and season.

3 Remove the chicken from the stock (keep that), and set aside.

4 For the tonnata sauce, whizz all the ingredients in a food processor with 2 tablespoons of water till smooth. Serve the chicken at room temperature, thinly sliced, with the sauce spooned on top, scattered with the capers and with the lemon potatoes.

Spinach & Ricotta Pasta Shells

This is an easy cheat's version of cannelloni, which I use as a starter or main. It has a soft, savoury stuffing that looks as pretty on the plate as it tastes great in the mouth.

For 3–4
Prep time
15 minutes
Cook time
10 minutes

All You Need Is...

250g dried conchiglioni
   pasta shells
   (large pasta shells)
200g baby spinach
150g ricotta cheese
good pinch of ground nutmeg

1 tbsp olive oil, plus
   extra for drizzling
100g Black Forest ham
   (smoked Parma ham)
25g Parmesan cheese,
   finely grated, to serve

All You Do Is...

1 Cook the pasta following the pack instructions. While it's bubbling away whizz the spinach, ricotta, nutmeg and the tablespoon of oil in a food processor till roughly combined. Grind in some pepper and add the ham. Give another quick whizz to roughly chop together.

2 Pop the filling in a small pan and gently warm through over a low heat. When the pasta is cooked, drain then toss in a drizzle of oil (just so the shells don't stick together). Stuff each shell with a small teaspoon of the spinach filling, then serve the stuffed pasta immediately with a generous drizzle of oil and a scattering of Parmesan.

Kids stuff
Tell 'em the green stuff is pesto...they'll love it.

Veggie option
The ham is definitely optional as it works well without.

Miso Noodle Broth
with Salmon

For 4
Prep time
5 minutes
Cook time
10 minutes

This delicious broth tastes like it's good for you. Well, it is good for you. It's what I call 'clean food' – fresh, tasty and healthy. I crave it when I've overindulged – if only I didn't shovel half a pound of chocolate in my mouth straight after.

All You Need Is...

4 individual miso
  soup sachets
3 tbsp light soy sauce
3 dried egg noodle nests
200g Tenderstem broccoli,
  roughly chopped

4 small salmon or trout
  fillets, boneless
  and skinned
handful of baby spinach

All You Do Is...

1 Empty the miso soup mix into a large saucepan, pour in 1 litre of boiling water, add the soy sauce, stir and bring to the boil.

2 Submerge the noodles and broccoli into the mix then sit the fish fillets on top. Cover and simmer for 4-5 minutes till the noodles are cooked and the fish is flaking.

3 Stir in the baby spinach, then serve in big bowls with chopsticks, spoons and paper napkins for wet chins.

Kids stuff
Very popular with my lot, and good for them too.

Italian Chicken Bake

For 4
Prep time
10 minutes
Cook time
35 minutes

One day the kids asked for pizza but I had planned to give them chicken. Thinking on my tired old feet I knocked up this delicious bake with all the Italian flavours they craved. I love it with salad and they... well, just love it.

All You Need Is...

1 onion, peeled and chopped
1 tbsp olive oil
3 free-range skinless chicken
  breasts, diced
2 garlic cloves, peeled and
  thinly sliced

2 tsp dried oregano
2 x 400g tins chopped
  tomatoes
1 x 125g ball mozzarella
  cheese, thinly sliced
50g sliced pepperoni

All You Do Is...

1 Preheat the oven to 180°C (fan), 200°C, gas mark 6. In a frying pan, fry the onion in the oil till translucent.

2 Add the diced chicken and fry, browning them for 5 minutes. Add the garlic and oregano and fry for 1-2 minutes before pouring in the tomatoes. Let it gently bubble for 5 more minutes.

3 Pop the lot into an ovenproof dish and top it first with the mozzarella then with the pepperoni.

4 Bake for 25 minutes till the pepperoni starts curling. Season and serve with warm garlic bread to soak up those yummy juices.

Baby biz
Whizz without the pepperoni.

Quick Fish Dish

For 4
Prep time
10 minutes
Cook time
35 minutes

Sometimes you need a fast easy way to turn that bit of fish into an exciting midweek treat – well this does exactly that...making a wet Wednesday rather wonderful.

All You Need Is...

1 onion, peeled and
   finely chopped
splash of olive oil
1 tsp ground cumin
2 x 400g tins chopped
   tomatoes
finely grated zest and juice
   of 1 orange

400g river cobbler or other
   firm white fish fillets, such
   as haddock or monkfish,
   skinned and boned
handful of fresh coriander,
   chopped

All You Do Is...

1 Fry the onion in the oil till cooked, about 5–10 minutes. Mix in the cumin, followed by the tomatoes and orange zest and juice, and simmer for 15 minutes.

2 Chop the fish into bite-sized pieces and add to the sauce. Now cover and simmer for another 15 minutes till the fish is cooked and starts to flake. Stir through the coriander. Serve with Lemon & Mint Couscous (see page 217), mash or rice and perhaps some steamed baby carrots.

Kids stuff and Baby biz
Check for bones.

Crusty Pistachio & Cranberry Salmon

This is easy, quick and impressively pretty. The sweet tasty crust means you can show off with it or just treat yourself midweek. Great with salads; I even love it cold.

For 4

Prep time
10 minutes

Cook time
20 minutes

All You Need Is...

2 tsp olive oil
4 tsp runny honey
4 salmon or trout fillets
  (about 150g each), skin on
60g shelled pistachios

40g dried cranberries
4 fresh rosemary sprigs,
  leaves only
2 garlic cloves, peeled

All You Do Is...

1 Preheat the oven to 180°C (fan), 200°C, gas mark 6. Mix the oil and honey together and drizzle half over the fish placed skinside down on a baking tray, spreading the mixture with the back of the spoon.

2 Whizz or finely chop the pistachios, cranberries, rosemary leaves and garlic cloves together. Mix with the other half of the oil and honey and pop the mixture on top of the fillets.

3 Bake for 15-20 minutes till the fish flakes and the crust is well...crusty. Season and serve with your favourite veg.

Baby biz
For very little ones just roast their fish in oil, honey and garlic till they can cope with the crunchy topping. (Take out the honey for the under one-year-olds.)

Golden Apricot Cake

For 8–10

Prep time
20 minutes

Cook time
55 minutes

Simply a lovely cake, the sticky golden syrup and pecan topping makes this a sponge cake with a warm apricot heart. It keeps really well and can also be a fabulous pudding with a few raspberries and a spoonful of crème fraîche on the side. This is what afternoon tea was invented for though...

All You Need Is...

180g butter, softened
180g golden caster sugar
3 large free-range eggs
180g self-raising flour, sifted
50g ground almonds
150g juicy ready-to-eat
   dried apricots, chopped

2 heaped tbsp apricot jam
4 tbsp golden syrup
100g pecans, broken up

Equipment
22–24cm springform cake tin

All You Do Is...

1 Preheat oven to 160°C (fan), 180°C, gas mark 4. Line the base of a cake tin with baking parchment.

2 Using an electric whisk, cream the butter and sugar together till fluffy, then beat in the eggs, one at a time with a spoonful of the flour.

3 Fold in the rest of the flour, the ground almonds and apricot pieces. Mix well and plop into the tin. Roughly smooth the top and bake for 45 minutes till golden and springy.

4 Meanwhile, mix the jam, golden syrup and pecans together then when the cake is ready spread the topping on and pop back in the oven for another 10 minutes. Take out and while still warm, loosen the edges of the cake from the tin. Serve with a cup of tea and a pinny on.

Passion Fruit Fairy Cakes

The tangy passion fruit twist on this classic teatime nibble gives these little cakes a sophistication that grown-ups love and kids wolf down... great for showing off at bake sales.

Makes
20–24

Prep time
10 minutes

Cook time
15–18 minutes

Freezable
(without icing)

All You Need Is...

200g caster sugar
200g butter, softened
200g self-raising flour
½ tsp baking powder
2 large free-range eggs
3 tbsp milk
finely grated zest of
   2 unwaxed lemons

Icing
10 tbsp icing sugar
3 passion fruit
juice of 1 lemon

Equipment
2 x 12-hole bun tins

All You Do Is...

1 Preheat the oven to 180°C (fan), 200°C, gas mark 6. Line the bun tins with 20–24 paper cases. Using an electric whisk, beat the sugar and butter together till fluffy. Add the flour, baking powder, eggs, milk and lemon zest and fold it all together well.

2 Plop a dessertspoonful of the mix into each paper case in the bun tins and bake for 15–18 minutes till golden. Leave to cool completely.

3 For the icing, mix the sugar and the pulp of the passion fruit together till it's thick and gloopy, and just dropping off the spoon. If you need to loosen it a touch use a drop or two of lemon juice. Dollop the icing on top of each cake and leave to set.

WEDNESDAY
FRIDAY WE
NERSHOP SID
TUESDAY WE

THURSDAY

KEND CORI
ES MONDAY
DNESDAY TI

Spanish Baked Beans

For 4
Prep time
10 minutes
Cook time
30 minutes
Freezable
(topping
only)

I could and do eat this till the cows home. That's no way to talk about my mum and auntie but they love it too. Serve with chicken or fish or just spoon it on toast with a drizzle of olive oil...Spanish old-school style.

All You Need Is...

1 red onion, peeled and
  finely chopped
80g chorizo, roughly chopped
splash of olive oil
small handful of fresh
  rosemary leaves, finely
  chopped
1 x 400g tin chopped
  tomatoes

2 x 400g tins butter beans,
  rinsed and drained

Topping
2 slices (100g)
  stale white bread
1 tbsp olive oil
½ tsp sweet smoked
  paprika

All You Do Is...

1 Preheat the oven to 180°C (fan) 200°C, gas mark 6. For the topping, blitz the bread, oil and paprika in a food processor into crumbs.

2 Fry the onion and chorizo in the oil for 5 minutes till they start to caramelise. Add the rosemary, tomatoes and beans and simmer for 5 minutes. Scrape the mixture into an ovenproof dish and top with the breadcrumbs.

3 Bake for 15–20 minutes till the top is golden and crunchy.

Other stuff
Up the paprika if you like a punch and cut out the Spanish pig if you want to go veggie.

Baby biz
Great whizzed without the chorizo or the topping.

Crispy Pesto Risotto Cakes

For 4

Prep time
10 minutes

Cook time
25 minutes
(plus cooling
and chilling)

You can serve these with everything from baby spinach with an egg on top to fish, lamb or chicken. However, I'm always trying to think of veggie options that will go down well with my meat-eating pride of man cubs, so I serve them with roasted veg.

All You Need Is...

1 onion, peeled and chopped
2–3 tbsp olive oil
250g risotto rice
800ml warm chicken or
  vegetable stock
2 tbsp fresh pesto (buy
  or make it, see page 214)

50g fresh breadcrumbs
25g Parmesan cheese,
  finely grated
2 knobs of butter

All You Do Is...

1 Make the risotto by frying the onion in a tablespoon of the oil till translucent. Pour in the rice and stir for 2 minutes to coat. Stir in the warm stock, a ladle at a time, letting the stock be absorbed before adding the next ladle and stirring. This should take about 20 minutes. When all the stock is absorbed the rice should be cooked but still have a little bite. Stir in the pesto, spread out onto a large plate or tray until cool and then cover and chill in the fridge for an hour or so.

2 Mix the breadcrumbs and Parmesan together. Scoop up dessertspoonfuls of the risotto and drop them into the crumbs, coating thoroughly, then gently press in your palm to form patties (this mix makes 8 good-sized ones). Leave in the fridge if you have time but it's not essential.

3 In a non-stick frying pan, melt a knob of butter with another tablespoon of the oil. Place half the patties in the pan and fry for 2–3 minutes, allowing them to crisp up, before gently flipping over and frying for another 2–3 minutes, but making sure they are heated right through. Repeat with the second batch. Rest on some kitchen paper then keep warm in a low oven if you need to. Season on the plate.

Time tip
Put your cakes together and store in the fridge overnight. If you have it, use any leftover risotto.

Sticky Marmalade Snags

They are sticky, they are sausages, what's not to like?

For 4
Prep time
5 minutes
Cook time
40 minutes

All You Need Is...

1 x 5cm piece fresh ginger,
   peeled and grated
1 heaped tsp grain mustard

2 heaped tbsp orange
   marmalade
1 x 12 pack British chipolatas

All You Do Is...

1 Preheat the oven to 180°C (fan), 200°C, gas mark 6.

2 Mix the ginger, mustard and marmalade together in a bowl. Chuck in the snags and toss to thoroughly coat.

3 Throw into an ovenproof dish and roast for 30-40 minutes till cooked through and looking yummy. Serve with all the sticky bits scraped off the base of the tin. This is great with Colly Stuffed Jackets (see page 173). Serve with wet wipes.

Sesame Beef
with Lime Noodles

These crispy beef morsels tossed through fresh lime noodles make a quick but unusual dish that my lot ask for by name...well they ask for 'the crispy noodley bite-sizey thingy thing' but I know what they mean.

For 4

Prep time
15 minutes
(plus marinating)

Cook time
15 minutes

Freezable
(raw, marinated, coated beef only)

All You Need Is...

300g sirloin steak,
   fat removed
2 tbsp plain flour
1 large free-range egg, beaten
100g sesame seeds
3 tbsp groundnut oil or olive oil

Marinade
1 tbsp light soy sauce
1 tbsp toasted sesame oil
finely grated zest and
   juice of 1 lime

1 tbsp peeled and finely
   grated fresh ginger
1 garlic clove, peeled
   and crushed

Lime Noodles
2 x 300g packs fresh
   egg noodles
splash of toasted sesame oil
handful of fresh mint leaves,
   chopped
grated zest and juice of 1 lime

All You Do Is...

1 In a bowl, mix all the marinade ingredients together. Slice the beef into finger-sized strips and mix with the marinade. Cover and chill for 30 minutes, or longer for a stronger flavour.

2 Drain the excess marinade then dip the beef strips, a couple at a time, first in the flour, then the egg, then finally the sesame seeds to coat. Lay on a plate and cover till ready to cook.

3 Fry your beef in the oil in two batches for 4–5 minutes, turning till golden on both sides. Set aside and keep warm. In a separate wok or frying pan, heat the noodles thoroughly in the oil, then dress with the mint and lime. Season and serve the beef with the noodles and some Tenderstem broccoli.

Time tip
Pre-prepare the raw sesame covered strips up to 24 hours in advance and keep in the fridge.

Baby biz
Great finger food, omit the soy for little babies.

Tangy Chicken & Squash Tray Bake

This has stood me in such good stead over the years. You can make it your own, be swayed by seasonal favourites or just throw in the bits and bobs from the bottom of the fridge. You are essentially roasting it all in a tangy, tasty dressing, which brings whatever is in the dish together.

For 4
Prep time
15 minutes
Cook time
45 minutes

All You Need Is...

8 free-range chicken thighs
1 butternut squash
2 tbsp olive oil
4 heaped tsp Dijon mustard

3 heaped tsp dried tarragon
finely grated zest and juice
of 1 unwaxed lemon

All You Do Is...

1 Preheat the oven to 180°C (fan), 200°C, gas mark 6.

2 Trim the fatty, flappy bits off the chicken thighs but leave some skin on. Deseed the squash and chop into bite-sized chunks. Throw in a large oven dish with the chicken thighs.

3 Mix the rest of the ingredients together, stir and cover the chicken and squash thoroughly in the mix, then bake for 45 minutes till golden and the chicken is cooked through. Season and serve with something green that excites you.

Other stuff
If squash is a challenge it also works brilliantly with aubergine, parsnips or parboiled potatoes.

Baby biz
Just whizz or chop some soft bits with a little stock.

Green Macaroni in Minutes

For 4

Prep time
20 minutes

Cook time
40 minutes

Freezable
(topping
only)

Macaroni cheese is the food equivalent of a pair of cosy bed socks – warm, soft and comforting on a cold winter's night. Well now those socks are green and fresh, so why wait for winter to try them on?

All You Need Is...

250g macaroni
2 big leeks, trimmed
   and chopped
splash of olive oil
100g frozen chopped spinach
1 x 125g ball mozzarella
   cheese
200g half-fat crème fraîche

1 tsp Dijon mustard
120g mature Cheddar
   cheese, grated

Topping
50g fresh breadcrumbs
25g Parmesan cheese,
   finely grated

All You Do Is...

1 Preheat the oven to 180°C (fan), 200°C, gas mark 6. Cook the macaroni following the pack instructions (the macaroni should be slightly undercooked).

2 Fry the leeks in the oil for 8–10 minutes till soft. Add the frozen spinach and gently cook till defrosted.

3 Take the pan off the heat, tear in the mozzarella and mix together with the drained pasta, crème fraîche, Dijon and Cheddar. Plop the mix into an ovenproof dish.

4 Now mix the breadcumbs and Parmesan together and sprinkle on top. Bake for 20 minutes till crispy and golden. Season and serve.

Time tip
It's a great one to make in the morning or day before. Leave in the fridge then bake (for 30 minutes if straight from the fridge) when you get home. Also look for the 3-minute express macaroni – it's a marvel.

Kids stuff
If they're scared of green food tell them it's pesto, if that doesn't work tell them it's kryptonite...I call it a little green lie.

Crispy Sage Lemon Sole with Garlic Butter

For 4
Prep time
10 minutes
Cook time
15 minutes

This delicate fish with garlic and lemon butter, sweetened by paprika and topped with crispy sage tastes like Italian holidays by the sea.

All You Need Is...

2 garlic cloves, peeled
  and squashed
50g butter
½ tsp sweet smoked paprika
juice of 1 lemon

4 sole fillets, skin on
  and boned
3–4 tbsp plain flour
2 big knobs of butter
16 fresh sage leaves

All You Do Is...

1 Pop the garlic in a small pan with the butter and paprika and heat until the butter has melted. Let it bubble gently for 1 minute, then add the lemon juice and heat for a further minute. Remove the garlic and keep warm.

2 Dust the fish in flour.

3 In a large non-stick frying pan, melt a big knob of butter and when hot, pop half the sage leaves in and fry for 2–3 minutes. Lay two fillets on top of the sage and fry flesh-side first.

4 Flip the fish and fry for a further 2–3 minutes till the skin is crisp and the flesh is flaking. Take out of the pan and repeat with the rest of the fish. Serve with the butter sauce poured over and some fresh new potatoes. Classic.

No-meat Meaty Lasagne

For 4–5
Prep time
20 minutes
Cook time
70–75
minutes
Freezable
(assembled
but unbaked)

Lasagne never fails to bring my family together to cries of 'yum, yum'. I make it the day before, and with the spinach it's a healthy wholesome Italian feast. The lentil sauce is fabulous on any pasta, so make extra and freeze it.

All You Need Is...

200g baby spinach
1 x 250g pack fresh or no-cook
   dried lasagne sheets
1 x 125g ball mozzarella cheese

White sauce
30g plain flour
30g butter
400ml milk
¼ tsp ground nutmeg

Lentil sauce
1 onion, peeled and finely chopped

1 carrot, peeled and finely chopped
1 celery stick, trimmed
   and finely chopped
splash of olive oil
1 garlic clove, peeled and crushed
80g red lentils, rinsed
2 tbsp tomato purée
1 x 400g tin chopped
   tomatoes
150ml vegetable or
   chicken stock

All You Do Is...

1 To make the lentil sauce, fry the onion, carrot and celery for 5 minutes in the oil. Add the garlic and fry for 1-2 minutes before throwing in the lentils, tomato purée, tomatoes and stock. Bring to the boil then turn down the heat, pop a lid on and simmer for 15 minutes.

2 Preheat the oven to 180°C (fan), 200°C, gas mark 6. To make the white sauce, place the flour, butter and milk in a small saucepan and whisk continuously together over a medium heat until thickened and smoothed. Add the nutmeg and simmer gently for a minute.

3 Meanwhile, pop the spinach in a pan with the lid on and gently cook for about 5 minutes. Put the spinach in a sieve and squeeze out the excess liquid.

4 To assemble, spread 2 tablespoons of the lentil sauce into the base of an ovenproof dish (about 22 x 26cm). Lay two pasta sheets on top, side by side, then spread 2 tablespoons of the lentil sauce and 2 tablespoons of the white sauce over the pasta. Now scatter all the spinach over the top, then repeat the pasta and sauce layering as before till you have used up all the ingredients, finishing with the white sauce.

5 Tear over the mozzarella and bake for 35 minutes till golden and bubbling. Season and serve.

Salmon with Pea Sauce

I pat myself on the back quite regularly but never more so than when I knock up a dish for a hungry crowd that looks like I've spent hours reducing and marinating, when in fact I've had a bath and spent half an hour surfing the internet for cellulite treatments. So go on, give yourself a pat on the back.

For 4
Prep time
10 minutes
Cook time
20 minutes

All You Need Is...

150ml vegetable stock cube
180g frozen peas,
   plus extra for serving
handful of fresh mint leaves
2 tbsp half-fat crème fraîche

4 salmon or trout fillets,
   skin on
100g pancetta cubes
2 garlic cloves, crushed

All You Do Is...

1 In a bowl, pour hot vegetable stock over the frozen peas and cover. After 5 minutes whizz in a food processor with most of the mint until smooth. Heat gently in a pan. When warm, add the crème fraîche and leave over a low heat.

2 In a non-stick frying pan, dry fry the pancetta until golden, adding the garlic at the end for 1 minute. Remove the pancetta and garlic with a slotted spoon and set aside.

3 Fry the salmon skinside down in the fat left from the pancetta for 10-12 minutes (depending on the thickness) turning halfway through. When the skin is crispy and the fish lightly cooked, pop on a plate, pour the pea sauce around it, scatter over the pancetta and garlic and a few saved mint leaves, finely chopped.

4 Season and serve with extra peas scattered over. Great with mash.

Time tip
Make the sauce up to one day ahead.

Baby biz
Check for bones.

Masala Chicken with Minty Rice

For 4
Prep time
15 minutes
Cook time
30 minutes
Freezable
(curry only)

This is a gentle way to introduce those wonderful Indian flavours to all the family, whatever age. Do add some fresh chilli if you want to hot it up!

All You Need Is...

1 onion, peeled and
  finely chopped
1 tbsp vegetable oil
2 tsp garam masala
1 tsp ground cumin
1 tsp ground ginger
2 garlic cloves, peeled
  and crushed
500g free-range skinless
  chicken breast, cut into
  bite-sized pieces

1 x 400g tin chopped
  tomatoes
1 tbsp sultanas
2 tbsp natural Greek yoghurt
50g toasted flaked almonds

Minty Rice
300g white basmati rice,
  rinsed
30g fresh mint leaves,
  chopped

All You Do Is...

1 In a large non-stick frying pan, cook the onion in the oil for 5 minutes. Add the three spices and the garlic and cook for another minute or two then throw in the chicken pieces, stirring for another 5 minutes.

2 Next, add the tomatoes and sultanas, pop the lid on and simmer for 20 minutes. Meanwhile, pop the rice in a saucepan with enough water to cover up to the first joint on your thumb, about 2.5cm above the rice. Bring to the boil, cover tightly with foil then turn down the heat and simmer for 5 minutes. Take off the heat and leave alone for a further 10 minutes. Uncover, fluff up with a fork, stir in the mint and serve.

3 Check the chicken is cooked through then take off the heat and stir in the yoghurt. Season and serve on the minty rice with flaked almonds sprinkled over the top.

One-minute Strawberry Fool

Kids and bigger humans alike will lick this bowl clean. One minute
to make, one minute to eat and potentially no washing up...

For 4
Prep time
1 minute

All You Need Is...

200g ripe strawberries, plus
  extra to decorate

1 x 500g pot fresh custard
fresh mint sprigs (optional)

All You Do Is...

1 Roughly chop the strawberries then mash them with a fork.
2 Mix with the custard, then serve in small glasses with a few extra
  strawberries on top and a sprig of mint if you are trying to posh it up.

Other stuff
Use any berries in season. Cooked gooseberries or rhubarb are amazing too.

Little Greek Almond Moons

Makes
about 20

Prep time
15 minutes

Cook time
15–18 minutes

Freezable

Fun to make with the kids and great to serve with ice cream or coffee, these remind me of old-fashioned petit fours. As the deep almond sweetness melts in my mouth, I'm transported back to teatime in posh London hotels where I would visit my posh London granddad. He'd wear a pinstripe suit and I'd wear my red velvet hand-me-down dress and shiny patent shoes. I like eating them and I like remembering.

All You Need Is...

200g ground almonds
140g caster sugar
2 large free-range egg whites

½ tsp almond extract
80g flaked almonds
icing sugar, for dusting

All You Do Is...

1 Preheat the oven to 180°C (fan), 200°C, gas mark 6. Line a large baking tray with baking paper.

2 Mix the ground almonds and sugar together. In another bowl, whisk the egg whites with the almond extract to soft peaks. Now fold the two mixtures together gently to form a soft dough.

3 With damp hands, roll a small teaspoon of the dough into little logs, then roll each one gently in the flaked almonds and bend into a crescent moon.

4 Pop on the lined tray and bake for 15–18 minutes till lightly golden. Cool slightly before easing off the paper. Once cool dust with icing sugar.

Storage stuff
These little moons can be kept for 2–3 days in an airtight container.

SDAY THURS
WEEKEND C
SIDES MOND
WEDNESDAY

FRIDAY

Chinese Duck Wraps

For 4
Prep time
5 minutes
Cook time
60 minutes

Some of my first birthday memories were from the posh Chinese restaurant at the end of my road. The Peking duck wraps were so fun to assemble and even now the sweet crunch of that crispy skin makes me feel six again. My own kids crave this treat as much as I did; the only difference is that they have to fight me for it.

All You Need Is...

2 duck legs
½ cucumber, deseeded
6 spring onions, trimmed
1 x 75g bag watercress

8 medium tortilla wraps
  or flatbreads
Hoisin sauce, to serve

All You Do Is...

1 Preheat the oven to 220°C (fan), 240°C, gas mark 9. Pat the duck skin dry with kitchen paper. Scrunch up a large piece of foil, put in the middle of an oven tray as a platform and pop the duck legs on top, then grind over a little salt. Roast for 1 hour till the meat falls off the bone and the skin is crispy; set aside.

2 Meanwhile, slice the cucumber and spring onions into matchsticks. Roughly chop the watercress then when the duck is slightly cooled strip the meat and crispy skin off the bones into small shredded pieces.

3 Put the wraps in foil and pop in the oven to gently warm through. To serve, just lay out all the ingredients on a platter and let everyone make their own. A teaspoon of Hoisin sauce spread over the wrap, followed by a little of everything else.

Kids stuff
Ducks. If you've just come back from feeding them and don't want to eat them, then chicken legs work well too.

Baby biz
Whizz or flake some duck and watercress with a little cooked potato and stock.

Ripley's Rack

For 4

Prep time
10 minutes

Cook time
80 minutes

Freezable
(simmered
ribs only)

I asked my butcher for his tip on ribs. My butcher asked the chef from the Thai restaurant opposite who had asked his mother who had taught him everything he knew. The secret is in the pineapple juice, which sweetens and tenderises the meat ready for my special sauce. I've always been proud of my rack and now you'll know why…

All You Need Is…

1 rack of baby back or loin
   British pork ribs
   (about 1kg)
juice of 1 lemon
300ml pineapple juice

Sauce
4 tbsp light soy sauce
3 garlic cloves, peeled
   and crushed

2 tbsp runny honey
2 tbsp sweet chilli sauce
2 tbsp tomato ketchup
1 tsp Thai 7 spice
1 x 5cm piece fresh ginger,
   peeled and grated

Equipment
Large 5–6 litre saucepan

All You Do Is…

1 Cut the ribs in half and put them in your largest saucepan with the lemon and pineapple juices. Cover with water, bring to the boil and pop the lid on. Turn down the heat and simmer for 20 minutes, then remove and drain.

2 Preheat the oven to 160°C (fan), 180°C, gas mark 4. Pop all the sauce ingredients in a small pan and heat gently, stirring, till it just bubbles. Set aside.

3 Lay the drained racks in a large roasting tin and cook in the oven for 40 minutes. Smear over half the sauce, then put back in the oven for 10 minutes before finally flipping the racks, smearing over the rest of the sauce and putting back in the oven for 10 more minutes. Remove and rest for 5 minutes. Cut into individual ribs, scrape up all the sauce you can and serve with my Egg-fried Rice (see page 219) and wet wipes.

Time tip
Pre-make the sauce.

Kids stuff
Wait till they have a good set of gnashers.

Smoked Mackerel Mexican Tacos

My husband is mad for Mexican, so this is my light, fresh and healthy nod to those clever amigos; olé!

For 4

Prep time
15 minutes

Cook time
None

All You Need Is...

1 x 400g tin black beans, rinsed and drained
juice of 1 lime
1 tbsp olive oil
2 ripe avocados, peeled, stoned and chopped

1 x 150ml pot soured cream
8 corn taco shells
100g baby spinach
2 tomatoes, chopped
250g smoked mackerel, skinned and flaked

All You Do Is...

1 Mix the beans, lime juice and oil togethor in a bowl crushing gently with a fork just to break the beans up.

2 In another bowl, again with a fork, roughly mash the avocados, then add the sour cream and mix to combine.

3 To load the tacos first layer a few spinach leaves, then a spoonful of the beans, the tomatoes, mackerel and lastly a spoonful of the avocado dressing. I fill bowls with all the ingredients and any leftovers, frankly, and let everyone make their own...

Whole Harissa Roast Fish

For 4
Prep time
5 minutes
Cook time
25 minutes

Cooking whole things, rather than bits of it, makes me feel very grown up, perhaps because it can look me straight in the eye – there is no hiding from the gaze of your dinner on a plate. The creamy yoghurt keeps the fish moist and the harissa and lime give it a zing – a great combo however old you're feeling.

All You Need Is...

2 whole sea bream or sea bass (about 300–350g each), gutted, cleaned and scaled

4 tbsp natural yoghurt
2 tsp harissa paste
2 limes

All You Do Is...

1 Preheat the oven to 200°C (fan), 220°C, gas mark 7. Place the fish on baking parchment in a roasting tray.

2 Mix the yoghurt and harissa together. Thinly slice half the lime, then fill the fish cavity with it and pop the other half next to the fish. Do the same with the second fish. Now cover each one in the yoghurt mix, leaving the head free.

3 Roast for 25 minutes till the fish flakes easily off the bone. Squeeze over the lime halves and serve. It's just great with my Nutty Mango Rice Salad (see page 70).

Kids stuff
Reduce the harissa by half first time to gauge how hot you can go.

Baby biz
Do one fillet without the harissa and be careful of bones.

Sweet Sticky Chicken

A sweet sticky treat that actually makes my kids love me more. In fact, I fear they would be slightly indifferent to me if this dish was not regularly on the menu. But if that's what it takes...

For 4
Prep time
15 minutes
Cook time
50 minutes

All You Need Is...

8 large free-range skinless, boneless chicken thighs
1 onion, peeled and chopped
splash of olive oil
2 garlic cloves, peeled and crushed

50ml light soy sauce
100ml chicken stock
100g light brown soft sugar
25g sesame seeds

All You Do Is...

1 Preheat the oven to 180°C (fan), 200°C, gas mark 6. Cut your chicken thighs in half.

2 In a large frying pan, fry the onion in the oil for 5 minutes then throw in the chicken to brown lightly all over for another 5 minutes. Add the garlic and fry for just 1 minute, then put them all into a baking tray or shallow ovenproof dish and pour over the soy sauce.

3 In the juices of the same frying pan, pour in the stock and let it bubble for a minute or two to release any leftover goodies in the pan. Pour it over the chicken and bake for 20 minutes.

4 Stir in the sugar and sesame seeds and bake for a further 20 minutes till the chicken is cooked. It's great with steamed broccoli dressed with lime and my Egg-fried Rice (see page 219).

Time tip
Get your butcher to do the hard work with the thighs – skin 'em, bone 'em and snip 'em in half.

Baby biz
When very wee just roast their chicken in a little of the oil, onion, stock and sesame seeds.

Nonna's Veal Marsala

For 4
Prep time
5 minutes
Cook time
8 minutes

My stepdad Ferro is Italian and belonged, like all good Italian boys, to a feisty Italian Mama known as Nonna. I was still very young when she passed away but I remember her wonderful veal marsala as if it were yesterday. This is my tribute to her and all other feisty Italian ladies who have their sons firmly tied to their nylon apron strings.

All You Need Is...

4 small British veal escalopes
   (about 100g each)
3 tbsp plain flour, for dusting
splash of olive oil

knob of butter
100ml sweet Marsala wine
2 lemons

All You Do Is...

1 Lay an escalope in between two pieces of cling film and, with a rolling pin, bash out till it is as thin as you can, about 2–3mm. Repeat with each piece of veal, then dust in the flour.

2 In a large non-stick frying pan, heat the oil over a high heat and fry the veal for 1–2 minutes on each side. Take out and cover with foil.

3 Throw the knob of butter into the pan and melt, then pour in the Marsala. Let it bubble and burn off for 2–3 minutes. Pop the veal back in to coat, then put on a plate and pour over all the lovely juices. Season and serve with a good squeeze of lemon juice and Little Italian Roasties (see page 216).

Time tip
Bash and flour the veal then pop in the fridge till you're ready to serve.

Baby biz
Although the alcohol burns off, just don't give the little ones the booze.

Poached Pesto Sea Bass on Summer Spaghetti

This dish was inspired by a recipe cooked for me on the telly by a posh chef. I have just made it easier and more family friendly but it still has that impressive restaurant vibe so feel free to charge for this one.

For 4

Prep time
25 minutes

Cook time
15 minutes

Freezable (uncooked sea bass in cling film only)

All You Need Is...

6 tbsp fresh pesto (buy or make it, see page 214)
4 tbsp fresh breadcrumbs
4 sea bass fillets (about 170g each), skinned
300g dried spaghetti
25g bunch of fresh mint leaves

25g bunch of fresh basil
2 tinned anchovy fillets
1½ tbsp capers
1 garlic clove, peeled and crushed
5 tbsp olive oil
1 tbsp white wine vinegar

All You Do Is...

1 Mix the pesto and breadcrumbs together. Lay a sea bass fillet in the middle of a large piece of cling film and spoon on a quarter of the pesto mix. As best you can, roll the fish up like a sleeping bag, then fold over the cling film and roll it up tight, twisting the ends to seal. Pop this parcel into a piece of foil, rolling again and twisting the ends like a cracker, then bring them up to make a handle. When ready, pop the parcels in boiling water and simmer for 15 minutes till firm. Take out of the water but keep wrapped till ready to serve.

2 Cook the pasta following the pack instructions, then drain. Now whizz or finely chop the mint, basil, anchovies, capers and garlic. Add the oil and vinegar then toss the dressing through the cooked pasta.

3 Unwrap the tubes of fish, slice them into three pieces and serve on top.

Time tip
Roll up the fillets ready to poach and keep in the fridge till needed. Make the dressing in advance too.

Other stuff
It sounds harder than it is!

Quick Thai Fish Curry

For 4
Prep time
5 minutes
Cook time
25–30
minutes

Sometimes you just fancy these warm exotic flavours. This short-cuts the time spent on a traditional curry but retains its spirit. Up the chilli if that lights your fire...

All You Need Is...

1 onion, peeled and finely
   chopped
splash of olive oil
2 tsp red or green mild
   Thai curry paste
1 x 400ml tin light
   coconut milk
100ml chicken stock

1 x 5cm piece fresh ginger
4 sea trout, salmon or pollack
   fillets, skinned
200g broccoli florets
handful of fresh coriander
¼ red chilli, finely chopped
1 lime, to serve

All You Do Is...

1 In a large frying pan, cook the onion in the oil for 10 minutes. Stir in the curry paste and cook for a minute before adding the coconut milk and stock, then finely grate in the ginger. Bring to the boil, turn down the heat and simmer for 5 minutes.

2 Chop the fish into big bite-sized pieces and add to the broth along with the broccoli. Pop a lid on and let it bubble for 5–10 minutes till the fish is flaking. Scatter the curry with coriander and chilli and serve in a big bowl with lots of rice and lime wedges.

Kids stuff
Either leave out the chilli or introduce a little as they get older.

Other stuff
Keep the ginger in the freezer as it's so much easier to grate.

Sweet Lamb Stew

For 4
Prep time
20 minutes
Cook time
50 minutes
Freezable

Producing this rich, tender stew on a winter's night will make you feel like a 'proper' home-maker. The kind that wears a pinny, bakes their own bread and helps with the war effort. The sweetness from the prunes will lure in the kids but be warned: the aromas from the pot may lure in the neighbours.

All You Need Is...

600g lamb leg steaks
1 tbsp olive oil
1 large red onion,
    peeled and chopped
80g cubed pancetta
1 tsp ground ginger

½ tsp ground cinnamon
400ml lamb stock
2 big tsp redcurrant jelly
100g soft pitted prunes,
    roughly chopped

All You Do Is...

1 Cut the lamb into bite-sized chunks, discarding any fat. In a heavy-based casserole dish, heat the oil, then brown the lamb in two batches for 2-3 minutes. Set aside.

2 Fry the onion and pancetta in the meat juices for 3-4 minutes. Stir in the ginger and cinnamon then add the stock and redcurrant jelly. Put the lamb back in and bring to the boil. Throw in the prunes, turn down the heat, pop on a lid and let it bubble gently for 30 minutes. Season and serve with classic mash potato.

Baby biz
Whizz or chop into mashed potato.

Crispy Prawn Salad

Prawns and sweet paprika belong together. This fresh tasty salad will delight and surprise all of you. It's my favourite summer lunch – even in winter.

For 3–4
Prep time
10 minutes
Cook time
6 minutes

All You Need Is...

2 level tbsp cornflour
1 tsp sweet smoked paprika
2 garlic cloves, peeled
  and crushed
280g raw peeled king prawns
2 tbsp sunflower oil

Salad
200g baby spinach
2 ripe avocados, peeled,
  stoned and chopped
2 large tomatoes, chopped
glug of olive oil
juice of 1 lime

All You Do Is...

1 Toss the spinach, avocados and tomatoes together and dress with the olive oil and lime juice.

2 Mix the cornflour, paprika and garlic together in a bowl. Pat the prawns dry with kitchen paper then toss thoroughly in the flour mixture to coat.

3 Heat the sunflower oil in a large non-stick frying pan then pop the prawns in for 2–3 minutes on each side. Flip over when crispy, then pop on a piece of kitchen paper to drain. Do this in two batches if necessary. Season and serve the prawns on top of the salad.

Easy Bakewell Cake

I'm such a big fan of the Bakewell that I once dragged my husband to the town of Bakewell in the Peak District just to taste their authentic tarts. Well mine is just as good but super easy to make. Serve warm with a scoop of vanilla ice cream or sneak a slice with a hot cup of coffee.

For 6–8

Prep time
15 minutes

Cook time
50 minutes

All You Need Is...

150g butter, softened
150g golden caster sugar
150g self-raising flour
150g ground almonds
2 large free-range eggs
1 tsp vanilla extract

6 tsp raspberry jam
1 x 150g punnet raspberries
50g flaked almonds

Equipment
22–24cm springform cake tin

All You Do Is...

1 Preheat the oven to 160°C (fan), 180°C, gas mark 4. Line the cake tin with baking parchment.

2 Using a food processor or an electric whisk, blitz or whizz the butter, sugar, flour, ground almonds, eggs and vanilla extract. Plop half of the mix into the lined cake tin and smooth.

3 Now dot the jam, ½ teaspoon at a time, all over and scatter with the raspberries. With the remainder of the cake mix, drop dollops over the fruit to cover but don't worry about the holes just use your fingers to spread it about a bit.

4 Scatter the flaked almonds over and bake for 45–50 minutes until golden brown. Serve warm or at room temperature.

Storage stuff
Leftovers make a great trifle base.

Easy Lemon & Raspberry Tart

For 6–8
Prep time
20 minutes
Cook time
50 minutes

I admit I'm addicted to lemons. I don't see it as a problem, although my husband Dan has flagged up that 'there are three of us in this relationship and one of us has got to go'. Well I can't make this quick and impressive tart without them so I've bought Dan a long stick and a large hanky. Now it's up to him.

All You Need Is...

1 x 375g pack sweet pastry
   (or make it, I dare you)
3 medium free-range eggs
75g caster sugar
220ml double cream
finely grated zest and juice of
   3 unwaxed lemons

200g fresh raspberries
icing sugar, for dusting

Equipment
24cm loose-bottomed flan tin
Baking beans

All You Do Is...

1 Preheat the oven to 180°C (fan), 200°C, gas mark 6. Roll out the pastry and use to line the flan tin. Cover the pastry with baking paper then fill with baking beans or rice and blind bake for 15 minutes. Remove the paper and beans then pop back in the oven for 5 minutes to dry out.

2 Reduce the oven temperature to 160°C (fan), 180°C, gas mark 4.

3 Whisk the eggs, sugar, cream, lemon zest and juice together. Leave the tin in the oven on a baking tray and scatter the raspberries over the base evenly. Pour the filling over the berries and bake for 30 minutes. Cool and maybe dust with icing sugar just before serving.

SDAY FRIDAY
CORNERSHO
DAY TUESDA
AY THURSDA

WEEKEND

SIDES MON
WEDNESD
FRIDAY W

Sesame Eggy Bread with Smoked Salmon

For 2

Prep time
5 minutes

Cook time
5 minutes

When I've got no time and very little in the fridge, I fall back on this because it delivers a tasty nutritious breakfast, brunch, lunch or light dinner in minutes. It looks pretty enough to eat, which is handy. That toasted sesame coating turns eggy bread into a surprise feast for everyone, and swapping the salmon for smoked mackerel also makes me slightly giddy with excitement.

All You Need Is...

splash of olive oil
knob of butter
2 large slices rustic bread
1 large free-range egg,
    whisked

2 tbsp sesame seeds
2 thick slices smoked salmon
1 lemon, cut into wedges
creamy horseradish sauce,
    to serve

All You Do Is...

1 Heat the oil and butter in a frying pan. First dip both sides of the bread in the egg then in the sesame seeds then fry for 3–4 minutes, turning once till golden. Drain on kitchen paper.

2 Serve with salmon on top, a good squeeze of lemon and a dollop of creamy horseradish.

Baby biz

Yummy finger food.

Now That's a Fry Up

Brunch or tea, this is tasty and quick. There are only a few ready-prepared veg bags I like and this is one of them. It's a great standby supper.

For 2
Prep time
5 minutes
Cook time
10 minutes

All You Need Is...

¼ French stick
2 tbsp olive oil
80g cubed pancetta
15g (small handful) fresh
  sage leaves, chopped

1 x 240g bag ready shredded
  cabbage and leek
2 large free-range eggs

All You Do Is...

1 Preheat the oven to 160°C (fan), 180°C, gas mark 4. Tear the bread into bite-sized pieces and toss in the oil with your hands. Bung in the oven for 10 minutes till crisp and golden.

2 Meanwhile, in a large frying pan, fry the pancetta in a tablespoon of the oil till crispy. Add the sage for a minute then the veg and fry till cooked and starting to crisp, about 10 minutes.

3 Poach or fry an egg to top the cabbage mix and throw over some croûtons to serve.

Other stuff
Also a great veggie option minus the pig, obviously.

Baby biz
Hard-boil the egg.

Fillet of Beef Caesar Salad

For 4
Prep time
15 minutes
Cook time
20 minutes

Great salads really ring my bell and this one is a tribute to the salad capital of the world, New York City. It will work for a dinner or lunch party as well as a special treat just for you. Present it on a large flat plate for maximum Big Apple pizzazz.

All You Need Is...

1 French stick
2 tbsp olive oil, plus extra
   for cooking
4 slices Parma ham
400g runner beans, trimmed,
   stringed and sliced
250g piece of fillet beef
1 x 240g bag baby spinach
20g Parmesan cheese

Dressing
4 anchovy fillets
2 tbsp light mayo
½ tbsp Dijon mustard
juice of 1 lemon
5 tbsp olive oil
1 garlic clove, peeled
   and crushed

All You Do Is...

1 Preheat the oven to 180°C (fan), 200°C, gas mark 6. Tear the bread into bite-sized pieces and toss in the oil with your hands. Bung in the oven for 10 minutes till crisp and golden. At the same time, lay the ham flat on a baking tray and roast for 10 minutes. Leave both to cool and crisp up.

2 For the dressing, squash the anchovies with the back of a knife, then finely chop and whisk with 1 tablespoon of water and the rest of the dressing ingredients.

3 Throw the beans into a pan of boiling water for 2 minutes then refresh under cold running water and drain.

4 Heat a splash of oil in a hot frying pan, pop the fillet in and fry for 4 minutes on each side. If it's a little pink for you just finish it in the oven for another few minutes. Rest the fillet for 5 minutes, then slice. To assemble the salad, toss the spinach and beans in 3–4 tablespoons of the dressing, then toss in the croûtons. Crumble over the crispy ham, scatter over the beef slices and, using a vegetable peeler, shave over some Parmesan. Season and serve with the extra dressing on the side.

Time tip
Make the dressing and croûtons, roast the ham and blanch the beans all in advance then just throw it all together at the last minute.

Other stuff
A cheaper cut like sirloin would work too.

Fig in a Pig on Garlic Bruschetta

For 4
Prep time
5 minutes
Cook time
10 minutes

When I throw a lunch or dinner party, I often struggle to think of a first course that's light, delicious, hassle free and only takes minutes to prepare. Well, problem solved – a perfect starter or light lunch for great first impressions.

All You Need Is...

4 ripe figs
4 knobs of Taleggio cheese
  (or any strong soft cheese)
4 slices Parma ham
4 slices rustic bread

1 garlic clove, peeled
  and halved
drizzle of olive oil, plus
  extra to serve
rocket leaves, to serve

All You Do Is...

1 Preheat the oven to 200°C (fan), 220°C, gas mark 7. Cut a deep cross through the top of the fig, keeping it intact at the bottom.

2 Push a knob of cheese into the middle and roll it up in a slice of ham with the top peeping out. Roast for 10 minutes.

3 For the bruschetta, griddle or toast the bread. While still hot, rub with the garlic halves and drizzle over the oil. To serve just scatter some rocket on top of the bruschetta and pop a pig on. Drizzle with a little more oil.

Roasted Butternut Squash Salad

Squash is one of nature's little miracles. By just roasting its warm, dense flesh you unlock that sweet sticky flavour. Enjoy with everything from fish, fowl, pasta, barbies, roasts and on and on and on...

For 4
Prep time
10 minutes
Cook time
60 minutes

All You Need Is...

70g pine nuts
1 butternut squash
  (about 1kg), unpeeled
20g fresh sage leaves
2 tbsp olive oil

Dressing
2 tbsp olive oil
1 tsp Dijon mustard
juice of 1 lemon
1 tsp runny honey

All You Do Is...

1 Preheat the oven to 180°C (fan), 200°C, gas mark 6. Toast the pine nuts on a baking tray in the oven for 10 minutes (don't forget them).

2 Cut the squash in half, deseed and chop it into big bite-sized pieces. Put the chopped squash in a large roasting tin, then tear in the sage leaves with 2 tablespoons of oil and toss. Roast for 45–50 minutes till cooked and just starting to get those yummy burnt toffee bits.

3 Whisk all the dressing ingredients together and toss through while still warm. Scatter over the toasted pine nuts. Serve warm or room temperature.

Time tip
I usually make this a few hours before. Keep covered at room temperature.

3 Top Dips

These dips are so versatile and don't take long to whip up. You can make them all in advance and keep covered in the fridge. They are my favourite starter for a dinner party as friends can tuck in while you sort out the main course. Fabulous for picnics or quick lunches served with lots of cut-up raw veg and pitta breads split in half horizontally and baked in the oven for 10 minutes till crisp.

Sweet Pepper Hummus

Prep time
10 minutes

All You Need Is...

1 x 400g tin chickpeas, drained
juice of 1 lemon
1 garlic clove, peeled and crushed
2 tbsp tahini paste

100g (about 3–4) roasted red peppers, from a jar
1 tbsp olive oil, plus extra to serve
sweet smoked paprika, to serve

All You Do Is...

1 In a food processor, whizz the lot with 1 tablespoon of water till smooth.

2 Serve with a pool of oil in the middle and a sprinkling of paprika.

Beetroot & Mint

Prep time
10 minutes

All You Need Is...

250g cooked beetroot,
   not in vinegar

100g soft goat's cheese
15g fresh mint leaves

All You Do Is...

1 In a food processor, whizz all three till smooth, holding back a couple of mint leaves to scatter on top.

Roasted Carrot with Feta

Prep time
10 minutes
Cook time
30 minutes

All You Need Is...

750g carrots, peeled and
   roughly chopped
3 tbsp olive oil
2 tsp ground cumin

120g natural yoghurt
30g fresh mint leaves
100g feta cheese,
   to serve

All You Do Is...

1 Preheat the oven 180°C (fan), 200°C, gas mark 6. Toss the carrots in 2 tablespoons of the oil and the cumin. Roast on an oven tray for 30 minutes, then leave to cool.

2 Whizz the cooled carrots, yoghurt, the remaining 1 tablespoon of oil and the mint (holding back a few leaves) in a food processor; don't over-whizz, keep it textured. Serve with the feta crumbled over with a few saved mint leaves.

Show-off Roast Chicken Platter

Roast chicken is still one of the great pleasures in life, along with foot rubs, new handbags and sleeping children. You can flavour your bird with spices and herbs from almost anywhere in the world: Thailand, India, France, Spain and, in this case, Morocco. It looks fabulous all laid out on a great big plate or board, tastes sublime and is delicious cold the next day.

For 6
Prep time
30 minutes
Cook time
125 minutes

All You Need Is...

100g pine nuts
1 whole free-range chicken
½ tsp ground cumin
½ tsp ground cinnamon
1 tbsp olive oil
1 lemon
1 x recipe Lemon & Mint
   Couscous (see page 217)

Aubergines
6 aubergines
4 tbsp olive oil

Tomato sauce
1 onion, peeled and
   finely chopped
1 tbsp olive oil
2 garlic cloves,
   peeled and crushed
1 tsp ground cumin
2 x 400g tins
   chopped tomatoes
handful of sultanas

Dressing
2 tbsp tahini paste
juice of 1 lemon

All You Do Is...

1 Preheat the oven 180°C (fan), 200°C, gas mark 6. Toast the pine nuts on a baking tray in the oven for about 10 minutes till just golden (don't forget them). Set aside.

2 In a roasting tray, dry the chicken skin with kitchen paper. Mix the cumin and cinnamon with the oil, then rub all over your bird. Cut the lemon in half and bung it inside the chicken with 2 tablespoons of water.

3 Roast till the juice runs clear, about 1 hour 15 minutes depending on the size of the chook (45 minutes per kg, plus 20 minutes). Rest, then carve all the meat off the carcass. Leave the oven on.

4 Once the chook's underway, chop the aubergines into fudge-sized chunks, toss in the oil and roast in a single layer in a large oven tray for 40 minutes.

5 While these are roasting, make the tomato sauce by frying the onion in the oil for 5 minutes. Add the garlic and fry for 1 minute, then add the cumin, tomatoes and sultanas and simmer, uncovered, for 15 minutes.

6 For the dressing, whisk the tahini paste with 4 tablespoons of water and the lemon juice.

7 To serve, on a large platter, first layer the Lemon & Mint Couscous, then the tomato sauce, followed by the aubergines, and then the cooked chicken. Drizzle the tahini dressing over the whole lot and sprinkle over the pine nuts. Season and serve with a huge green salad.

Time tip
You can pre-make the couscous, tomato sauce (just warm through when needed), the dressing and pre-roast the nuts and aubergines.

Kids stuff
The aubergines might appeal more to the adults, but that's good right?

Baby biz
Just whizz a bit of everything.

Beetroot & Horseradish Beefburgers

For 4
or more

Prep time
5 minutes

Cook time
15 minutes

Freezable
(raw)

This'll put hairs on your chest – a meaty feast with an earthy thrust. Beetroot's bright red flesh means it's tricky to judge the cooking time of the burgers, but if you're worried just let it sizzle away for a bit longer. I like mine fairly rare but that's because I'm a real man! Also brilliant on a barbie.

All You Need Is...

1 large raw beetroot, peeled

500g lean beef mince

4 tsp creamy horseradish sauce

splash of olive oil

All You Do Is...

1 Grate the beetroot into the beef and mix well with the horseradish. Season with a grind of salt and pepper and form into 8 patties with damp hands.

2 Heat the oil in a large non-stick frying pan and cook the burgers over a medium–high heat for about 7 minutes on each side for medium to well done. Serve with fries…you know you want to!

Time tip
Great made beforehand and kept in the fridge to firm up.

Other stuff
Wear rubber gloves to avoid staining your hands when grating the beetroot, unless it's Halloween!

Feta & Mint Roast Lamb

For 6
Prep time
15 minutes
Cook time
80 minutes

This lamb is fit for a queen and not just one of those with false eyelashes and hairy legs that pop round mine for a slap-up Sunday lunch; so simple and delicious yet a dish to show off with.

All You Need Is...

30g fresh mint leaves,
   chopped
finely grated zest of
   1 unwaxed lemon
5 garlic cloves, peeled

200g feta cheese
2 tbsp olive oil
1.5kg boneless shoulder
   of lamb

All You Do Is...

1 Preheat oven to 220°C (fan), 240°C, gas mark 9. For the stuffing, mix the mint, lemon zest and 2 crushed garlic cloves together. Crumble in the feta with a tablespoon of the oil and work it into a rough paste.

2 Cut a large opening through the middle of the lamb and push in all of the feta mix. Tie up with string like a parcel.

3 Cut the other 3 garlic cloves into slivers. Jab a sharp knife into the top of the meat (about 15 incisions) and push in the garlic pieces, then rub a tablespoon of oil into the flesh, and season.

4 Pop the lamb in a roasting tray, with a lemon cut in half alongside it. Bung in the oven for 20 minutes then turn the oven temperature down to 180°C (fan), 200°C, gas mark 6 and cook for 1 hour (medium pink), 20 minutes extra if you prefer it a little more done. Take out of the oven and squeeze the hot lemon juice over the lamb and rest for 15 minutes. Carve into chunky slices with the juices poured over. Season and serve with Rosemary Polenta Roasties (see page 212) and My Big Green Salad (see page 35).

Time tip
Pre-stuff your shoulder, then take out of the fridge half an hour before roasting.

Baby biz
Fabulous whizzed with a drop of stock and some veg.

My Big Savoury Pancake

This is a birthday special. I prep everything beforehand, ready to assemble, then cook and grandly bring to the table with a loud... 'Ta da!' It's a soft, smooth version of a lasagne with a celebratory feel.

Serves 4
Prep time
25 minutes
Cook time
35 minutes

All You Need Is...

8 large tbsp (leftover)
  Bolognese sauce
1 x 125g ball mozzarella
  cheese
grated Parmesan cheese,
  to serve

White sauce (make or buy)
30g butter
30g plain flour
300ml milk
¼ tsp ground nutmeg

Pancakes (make or buy)
110g plain flour
2 large free-range eggs
200ml milk mixed with
  75ml water
splash of olive oil

Equipment
24cm springform cake tin

All You Do Is...

1 For the white sauce, gently melt the butter in a pan, then while stirring with a wooden spoon add the flour to form a paste. Gradually pour in the milk, whisking constantly till it's smooth as custard and starts to thicken, about 3–4 minutes. Add the nutmeg and set aside.

2 For the pancakes, sift the flour into a bowl. Add the eggs and whisk to combine. Drizzle in the milk and water, whisking till it has the consistency of single cream. Lightly oil a large frying pan and heat. When hot, dollop in a ladleful (about 100ml) of batter, turning the pan to cover the base. Flip when the underside starts to bubble, pop on a plate, and repeat with the remaining the batter to make 5 pancakes.

3 Preheat the oven to 180°C (fan), 200°C, gas mark 6. Grease the cake tin and put a pancake on the base. Spread with 2 tablespoons of bolo sauce, followed by 2 tablespoons of white sauce drizzled over. Repeat with more cakes till the final one. Cover this with torn mozzarella and leftover white sauce. Pop in the oven to heat and brown for 20 minutes or so. Carefully release from the tin, slice and serve topped with Parmesan, and real or carrot candles if it's a celebration.

Time tip
You can pre-make and chill everything, assembling it all just before baking. Or, buy ready-made pancakes, white sauce and fresh ragu – whatever works for you.

Crackling Pork with a Sage & Apricot Tunnel

For 6
Prep time
15 minutes
Cook time
90 minutes

If you need to impress the mother-in-law, get yourself a boyfriend or win MasterChef, then roast this little piggy because it's the crown jewels of roast dinners. With its armour of crackling and sweet sage stuffing this will give you god-like status. I tell the kids the crackling is pig toenail to ensure I get a bigger helping.

All You Need Is...

1½ kg British pork loin (off
   the bone and scored by
   your butcher), skin on
1 tbsp olive oil

Stuffing
100g ready-to-eat
   dried apricots

100g Parma ham
50g pine nuts
15g fresh sage leaves
3 garlic cloves, peeled
2 unwaxed lemons

All You Do Is...

1 For the stuffing, whizz in a food processor or finely chop the apricots, ham, pine nuts, sage leaves, garlic and the zest of your lemons into coarse crumbs.

2 With a long, wide knife cut a tunnel through the middle of the pork loin without breaking through the outside wall. Go in from the other end so at least two fingers fit all the way through. Now pack that pig with your stuffing (fingers and the handle of a wooden spoon work best).

3 Place the pork on a roasting tray (if you have asked the butcher to keep the rack that the loin was cut from them pop it on top of that). Now leave at room temperature for 30 minutes or so to dry out. Pat the pork dry with kitchen paper.

4 Preheat the oven to 220°C (fan), 240°C, gas mark 9. Rub the pork first with the oil then with some salt.

5 Pop in the hot oven for 30 minutes then reduce the oven temperature to 180°C (fan), 200°C, gas mark 6 and roast for a further 1 hour till cooked and the juices run clear. Rest than carve into chunky slices, pour over any juices and serve with all the trimmings.

Time tip
Stuff in advance and leave uncovered in the fridge.

Colly Stuffed Jackets

I often forget about good old jacket potatoes, but there's little better on a dark autumn night than that husky crisp skin and fluffy white centre. The cauliflower stuffing oozes out, making this a meal in itself but the temptation to serve it with my Sticky Snags (see page 101) is sometimes too much to resist...

For 4
Prep time
15 minutes
Cook time
105 minutes

All You Need Is...

4 medium baking potatoes
1 small cauliflower
8 sun-blushed tomato pieces
 (about 50g), finely chopped

Cheese sauce
30g butter
30g plain flour
300ml milk
100g mature Cheddar cheese,
 roughly grated

All You Do Is...

1 Preheat the oven to 200°C (fan), 220°C, gas mark 7. Bake those spuds for 1–1½ hours, depending on their size, till soft on the inside and crispy on the outside.

2 Meanwhile, divide the colly into florets, then each floret into at least 4 bits and lightly cook in boiling water for 3–4 minutes. Drain and set aside.

3 Make the sauce by gently melting the butter in a pan then while stirring with a wooden spoon add the flour to form a paste. Gradually pour in the milk, whisking constantly till it's smooth as custard and starts to thicken, about 3–4 minutes. Throw in 70g of the Cheddar and stir till it melts, then set aside.

4 When the spuds are ready, cut them in half (ouch! hold with a tea towel), scoop out the soft flesh and bung about three-quarters of it in the cheese sauce along with the cooked colly and tomatoes.

5 Mix everything together then pile high back into the potato skins. Lastly, scatter the rest of the cheese on top. Pop back in the oven for 15 minutes to brown and bubble. Then season and serve.

Time tip
You can, of course, buy ready-made cheese sauce or make it beforehand and add the colly and tomatoes ready for the final stage.

Baby biz
Just mash the colly, sauce and potato flesh with a fork.

My Simple Sachértorte

For 8–10
Prep time
20 minutes
Cook time
35 minutes
(plus cooling)
Freezable
(without
topping)

At the start of the global recession I decided to cut back on some of life's luxuries to ease our financial burden. I started taking the bus more often, nagged 23 hours a day to 'TURN THE LIGHTS OFF!'. I even started darning socks, but how could I give up that oh-so-expensive slice of Sachertorte from my local cake shop? The answer was clear, make my own. Now I can have four slices for the same price, which probably is missing the point but I feel like I'm doing my bit. This is the best cake I make and I'm fully expecting it to get the economy back on its feet.

All You Need Is...

200g dark chocolate (at least
   70% cocoa solids), broken up
160g butter, softened
120g caster sugar
4 large free-range eggs,
   separated
200g ground almonds

Topping
100g dark chocolate (70%
   cocoa solids), broken up
50g butter
3 heaped tbsp apricot jam

Equipment
20–22cm springform cake tin

All You Do Is...

1 Preheat oven to 150°C (fan), 170°C, gas mark 3. Line the base of the cake tin with baking parchment. Melt the chocolate in a glass bowl set over a pan of simmering water, then set aside.

2 Using an electric whisk, cream the butter and sugar together till fluffy. Add the egg yolks, melted chocolate and ground almonds and mix until evenly combined.

3 In a separate bowl, whisk the egg whites with an electric whisk till soft peaks form, then carefully fold into the cake mix. Pop in the tin and bake for 35 minutes, then cool completely in the tin.

4 For the topping, melt the chocolate and butter in a glass bowl set over a pan of simmering water. Leave to cool slightly.

5 Carefully remove the cool cake from its tin then spread the jam over the top of the cake. Dribble over the warm chocolate topping, letting it drip down the sides a little and leave it to set. Serve at room temperature.

Storage stuff
Defo make the day before, if you can keep your hands off it.

Kids stuff
Hide it!

Blueberry & Coconut Cake

A magic, exotic match made in heaven: blueberries, coconut and almonds – both comforting and sexy at the same time. I'm clearly at the stage in my life where cake is sexy. Are you?

For 8
Prep time
20 minutes
Cook time
50 minutes

All You Need Is...

180g butter, softened
180g caster sugar
2 large free-range eggs
1 tsp vanilla extract
100g ground almonds
150g self-raising flour, sifted

60g desiccated coconut
300g fresh blueberries
crème fraîche and coconut
  cream, to serve

Equipment
22–24cm springform cake tin

All You Do Is...

1 Preheat the oven to 160°C (fan), 180°C, gas mark 4. Line the base of the cake tin with baking parchment. Using an electric whisk, cream the butter and sugar together till fluffy.

2 Add the eggs, vanilla and almonds and whisk again. Now fold in the flour and coconut to combine, then gently fold in the blueberries.

3 Scrape the mix into the tin, roughly smooth the top and bake for 50 minutes till golden and springy. Cool in the tin. Serve warm with a dollop of crème fraîche with a spoonful of coconut cream stirred through if you fancy.

Nutty Nuggets of Deliciousness

Makes
25–30

Prep time
20 minutes

Cook time
15 minutes

Freezable
(unassembled
biscuits only)

Make these and make them now, then write to me and thank me. In fact, write to the Queen and tell her to make me a dame because your world is about to get just a little bit better. I serve them at the end of a posh dinner with coffee but these little beauties will give a lift to a picnic, lunchbox or parties for any age. The only downside is that you may feel angry towards those who ask for more; hide some, I do.

All You Need Is...

100g whole blanched
  hazelnuts
100g ground almonds
150g plain flour

60g golden caster sugar
150g butter, softened
⅓ of a 400g jar Nutella

All You Do Is...

1 Preheat the oven to 180°C (fan), 200°C, gas mark 6. Line two baking trays with baking parchment. Spread the hazelnuts out on a roasting tray and bung in the oven for 8–10 minutes, or till lightly golden (don't forget them). Leave to cool slightly, then blitz the nuts in a food processor into fine crumbs.

2 Add the almonds, flour, sugar and butter to the food processor and whizz till it all comes together.

3 Roll little teaspoon-sized amounts of the mixture in your hands to make balls of dough the size of large marbles. Slightly flatten, then space out on the baking trays and bake for 15–20 minutes.

4 Cool completely on the trays then sandwich them together with a blob of Nutella. Store in the fridge and take out shortly before serving.

Time tip
These will last up to three days in an airtight container in the fridge.
You can save time and buy toasted hazelnuts, then blitz.

Kids stuff
Get little hands to help make little balls.

Sticky Orange & Date Cake with Butterscotch Sauce

For
10–12

Prep time
20 minutes

Cook time
60 minutes

Freezable
(sponge only)

My cake prayer: 'Thank you lord for this mostest moistest cake that makes me humble at the foot of my oven. Let it rise again and again and again for I am only truly complete with it in my belly.' Amen.

All You Need Is...

180g butter, softened
180g golden caster sugar
4 large free-range eggs
120g orange marmalade
200g spelt or wholemeal
   plain flour, sifted
50g ground almonds
1½ heaped tsp baking
   powder, sifted
finely grated zest and juice
   of 1 orange

150g dates, stoned
   and roughly chopped
100g sultanas

Sauce
50g butter
50g soft brown sugar
1 tbsp golden syrup
finely grated zest of 1 orange
100ml thick double cream

Equipment
24cm springform cake tin

All You Do Is...

1 Preheat the oven to 160°C (fan), 180°C, gas mark 4. Line the base of the cake tin with baking parchment.

2 Using an electric whisk, cream the butter and sugar together till fluffy. Whisk in the eggs, one at a time followed by the marmalade. Fold in the flour, almonds, baking powder, orange zest and half of the orange juice.

3 Fold in the dates and sultanas and plop the mix in the tin. Bake for 50–60 minutes till a skewer comes out clean.

4 Meanwhile, make the sauce by gently melting the butter, sugar and golden syrup with the orange zest and 1 tablespoon of the remaining orange juice in a small pan. When totally smooth, take off the heat and mix in the cream. Serve the cake still warm with the hot sauce or at room temperature with a cuppa.

Time tip
Pre-make the cake and sauce. Gently warm the sauce before serving.

So Good, So Easy, Sort-of Scones

These couldn't be easier to make and yet I feel like the perfect wife, mother and woman for producing such comforting teatime treats. Old-fashioned in the right way, they remind me of grandmas (of all grandmas, not just mine) as I sit with a cup of tea and make yet another pledge to start knitting that woolly scarf for my Dad.

Makes
8–10
Prep time
15 minutes
Cook time
20 minutes

All You Need Is...

300g plain flour
4 tsp baking powder
80g unrefined golden
  caster sugar
2 tsp mixed spice

180g butter, softened
150g sultanas
1 large free-range egg
50ml milk

All You Do Is...

1 Preheat the oven to 180°C (fan), 200°C, gas mark 6. Line a large baking tray with baking paper.

2 Mix the flour, baking powder, sugar and mixed spice together, then whizz it all in a food processor with the butter, or rub everything together with your fingertips till crumb-like. Plop the mixture in a bowl with the sultanas.

3 Separately whisk the egg and milk then fold everything together. Now put dessertspoon lumps of the sticky dough onto the lined baking tray and bake for 18–20 minutes till golden. Serve warm with butter and jam.

Other stuff

Warm through the next day – if any are left.

WEEKEND C
SIDES MOND
WEDNESDAY
FRIDAY WEE

CORNERSHOP

AY TUESDAY

THURSDAY

KEND CORN

Comforting Rice
& Garden Veg Soup

For 4
Prep time
15 minutes
Cook time
30 minutes

Simple, fresh flavours to warm the cockles of your heart and home, this is also delicious the next day as it basically turns into risotto. Just reheat it thoroughly and cover with some grated Parmesan.

All You Need Is...

2 leeks, trimmed and
  finely chopped
2 large carrots, peeled and
  finely chopped
splash of olive oil
Parmesan rind
¼ tsp ground nutmeg

120g risotto rice
1¼ litres chicken or
  vegetable stock
2 tbsp tomato purée
200g baby spinach
grated Parmesan cheese,
  to serve

All You Do Is...

1 In a very large saucepan, fry the leeks and carrots in the oil to soften. After 5 minutes throw in the Parmesan rind and cook for a further 5 minutes.

2 Now add the nutmeg and rice, stir, then add the stock and tomato purée. Pop a lid on and simmer for 20 minutes.

3 Finally, chuck in the spinach leaves, stir for 1 minute, then discard the rind. Serve with plenty of grated Parmesan.

Kids stuff
A healthy soup with all the flavours they love (just don't add the spinach if it's got a bad name in your house).

Rustic Italian
Savoury Scone Loaf

When someone produces home-baked bread I see them as more wholesome, of better character and of sweeter nature than the rest of us. But I am impatient and just can't be bothered to wait for that dough to rise. So I make this wonderful, quick rustic scone loaf, which you can serve with so many dishes from Peasant's Pasta e Fagioli (see page 196) to Fillet of Beef Caesar Salad (see page 152), with soups, or on a picnic. Guaranteed to make you look like a saint.

For
6–8
Prep time
10 minutes
Cook time
25 minutes
Freezable

All You Need Is...

250g self-raising flour
1 x 125g ball mozzarella
  cheese, roughly chopped
100g pitted black olives,
  halved
3 large free-range eggs

30ml olive oil
75g fresh pesto (buy or
  make it, see page 214)
2 small fresh rosemary
  sprigs

All You Do Is...

1 Preheat the oven to 200°C (fan), 220°C, gas mark 7. Line an oven tray with baking paper.

2 In a bowl, mix the flour with the mozzarella and olives. In a jug, whisk the eggs with the oil and pesto.

3 Make a well in the flour mixture, pour in the egg mix and fold it all together with a big metal spoon till it comes together into a loose, wetish dough ball.

4 Plop it onto the lined baking tray, moulding it roughly into a round ball, about 20cm, then just break off little clumps of rosemary and push them into the top of the loaf. Grind over plenty of sea salt and pop in the oven for 25 minutes till cooked. Rest for 5 minutes. Serve warm straight from the oven if possible. Reheat when needed.

Falafel Burgers

For 4
Prep time
15 minutes
Cook time
10 minutes
Freezable
(raw)

You are meant to deep-fry falafel really, but the deep-fat fryer my Auntie Twinkle gave me in the 80s has long since been confiscated by the heart-attack police. These mighty minty veggie burgers really hit the Middle Eastern mark for lunches, picnics or something different for dinner.

All You Need Is...

1 x 400g tin chickpeas,
    drained and rinsed
3 spring onions, trimmed
    and roughly chopped
20g fresh mint leaves
1 large carrot, peeled
    and grated
1 garlic clove, peeled
    and crushed
1 tsp ground cumin
½ tsp ground coriander

¼ tsp sea salt
2 tbsp plain flour, plus
    extra for dusting
2–3 tbsp olive oil

To serve
soft buns, or pitta breads
1 x 200g pot hummus (buy
    or make it, see page 158)
1 apple, cored and
    thinly sliced

All You Do Is...

1 Throw the chickpeas, spring onions, mint, carrot, garlic, spices, salt and flour in a food processor and whizz till smooth. With floured hands, form the mix into 8 flat patties.

2 In a large non-stick frying pan, heat the oil, then fry the burgers till golden and crispy, about 3–4 minutes on each side. Serve in small soft buns or pitta bread with a dollop of hummus and a couple of slices of apple.

Baby biz
Make theirs without the salt.

Quick Naan Pizza

For 2

Prep time
10 minutes

Cook time
25 minutes

I just didn't have time to make pizza dough, so shoot me! I did, however, rush into my cornershop and grab some naan bread. I topped it with all the Italian trimmings I could muster and found that the soft naan base worked brilliantly – a top tasty time saver.

All You Need Is...

2 plain naan breads
1 x 125g ball mozzarella
   cheese, sliced
6 slices salami
10 favourite olives

Quick tomato sauce
1 x 400g tin
   chopped tomatoes
1 tbsp balsamic vinegar
1 garlic clove, peeled
   and crushed
pinch of sugar

All You Do Is...

1 Mix all the tomato sauce ingredients together in a saucepan and bring to the boil. Turn down the heat and simmer for 10 minutes to reduce into a thick sauce.

2 When ready, preheat the oven to 200°C (fan), 220°C, gas mark 7.

3 Place the naan breads on a large non-stick baking tray and spread half the tomato sauce onto each naan, arranging the mozzarella, salami and olives on top.

4 Pop in the oven for about 15 minutes to crisp up.

Other stuff

This is just a basic topping but feel free to pop on all your favourites.

Cornershop Sardine Spaghetti

This is one of the tastiest pastas I make. A classic Italian combo that's just waiting in your store cupboard. It's bursting with flavour and good enough to serve to a crowd at lunchtime or whip up in a hurry.

For 4

Prep time
5 minutes

Cook time
10 minutes

All You Need Is...

3 slices stale bread
  (about 120g)
4 tbsp olive oil
300g dried spaghetti
2 x 120g tins sardines
  in olive oil, drained
large handful of fresh
  parsley, chopped

200g tin pitted green olives,
  chopped (anchovy-stuffed
  if available)
finely grated zest and juice
  of 1 unwaxed lemon

All You Do Is...

1 Whizz the bread in a food processor into crumbs

2 Heat 2 tablespoons of the oil and gently fry the breadcrumbs till golden.

3 Cook your pasta following the pack instructions, then drain.

4 Break up the sardines with a fork and mix with the drained spaghetti, parsley, olives, lemon zest and juice plus the remaining 2 tablespoons of oil. Sprinkle the breadcrumbs on top. Season and serve with a great salad.

Time tip
Use any stale ends of loaves and keep the breadcrumbs in the freezer ready.

Kids stuff
Start them early on oily fish for bright sparks with great hair!

Peasant's Pasta e Fagioli

For 4
Prep time
10 minutes
Cook time
25 minutes

This simple, comforting recipe is straight off a Tuscan hilltop, where my mum-in-law Patrizia cooks classic Italian fare. She calls it peasant food; some peasants have all the luck. I threw in the chorizo for a bit of bite and now this take on classic *pasta e fagioli* is fit for a king.

All You Need Is...

1 red onion, peeled and finely chopped
1 celery stick, trimmed and finely chopped
80g chorizo or streaky bacon, cubed
1 potato (about 100g), peeled
2 garlic cloves, peeled and crushed
500ml chicken stock

1 x 400g tin chopped tomatoes
100g small dried pasta like farfalle, baby pasta shells or broken up spaghetti
1 x 400g tin mixed beans (don't drain)
grated Parmesan cheese, to serve
olive oil, to serve

All You Do Is...

1 In a large saucepan, cook the onion, celery and chorizo for 5 minutes.

2 Chop the spud into very small cubes, about ½ a sugar cube. Add the pieces to the pan with the garlic and fry for a further 5 minutes.

3 Pour in the stock, tomatoes, pasta and the tin of beans, water and all. Give a good stir to get all the delicious stuff off the base of the pan, then pop a lid on and simmer for about 15 minutes till the potatoes are soft and the pasta is cooked through. Season and serve with a drizzle of oil and a sprinkle of Parmesan.

Other stuff
If using streaky bacon instead of the chorizo then fry the onion, celery and bacon in a little oil.

Pear Pudding

Old-school, comforting puddings that taste like Sundays – these are the memories we leave with our kids. I remember almost nothing from my childhood except tastes and smells; this soft, sweet, easy pudding makes me look back through pear-tinted glasses...

For 6
Prep time
20 minutes
Cook time
35 minutes

All You Need Is...

180g plain flour
1 heaped tsp baking powder
150g golden caster sugar,
   extra 1 tbsp for topping
3 large free-range eggs
2 tsp vanilla extract
60ml milk

150g butter, melted
2 x 400g tins pear halves
   in juice, drained

Equipment
Square ceramic ovenproof
   dish or brownie tin

All You Do Is...

1 Preheat the oven to 180°C (fan), 200°C, gas mark 6. Line the base of your dish or brownie tin with baking parchment. Sift the flour and baking powder into a bowl and add the sugar.

2 In a jug, beat the eggs, vanilla and milk together then whisk gently into the dry ingredients till completely combined, adding the melted butter last.

3 Pour the batter into the dish or brownie tin, then chop the pears and scatter all over. Pop in the oven for 35 minutes till firm and golden, sprinkling the extra sugar over halfway through cooking. Serve warm with custard, old, old school.

Other stuff
Also great with your favourite soft seasonal fruits.

Time tip
Use leftovers as a trifle base.

Lamingtons

Makes
20–25

Prep time
20 minutes

Cook time
45–50
minutes

Freezable
(sponge only)

Dan, my Aussie husband, seems to think that everything is an Australian invention. He reckons our Victorian architecture was copied from his homeland; that King's Cross was down under first and that the Queen is covering up an Aussie accent. Bless! Well, these fluffy sweet cakes make my hubby and kids squeal with delight. They are messy to make but definitely Antipodean and taste 'bonza to boot!'.

All You Need Is...

Sponge
230g butter, softened
250g caster sugar
1 tsp vanilla extract
4 large free-range eggs
250g self-raising flour, sifted

Coating
20g butter
200g dark chocolate
150g icing sugar
120ml milk
300g desiccated coconut

Equipment
30 x 20cm brownie tin

All You Do Is...

1 Preheat the oven to 160°C (fan), 180°C, gas mark 4. Line the base of the brownie tin with baking paper.

2 Using an electric hand whisk, cream the butter and sugar together in a large bowl till pale and fluffy. Add the vanilla then the eggs, one at a time. Now fold in the flour then, with a spatula, scoop the mix into the tin. Smooth out and bake for 40–45 minutes till a skewer comes out clean. Cool in the tin. Cut the cake into cubes (size is your call but I like mine big enough for two bites).

3 For the coating, pop the butter and chocolate in a glass bowl set over a pan of simmering water and, when melted, add the icing sugar and milk, stirring till smooth.

4 To coat, first dip each cake cube on all sides in the melted chocolate then roll in a separate bowl of the coconut. This is messy but the good news is that you get to lick your fingers; it's the law.

Kids stuff
It's fun to let them join in the coating stage.

Sultana Bran Crispies

Makes 12
Prep time
5 minutes
Cook time
5 minutes
(plus setting time)

Who knew that with so little effort you could create such moreish crunchy treats that adults will, when necessary, lie, cheat and inflict Chinese burns to get their hands on. So watch out kids, they're in the fridge...but not for long.

All You Need Is...

120g milk Toblerone, broken up

130g Sultana Bran

1 tbsp golden syrup

50g hazelnuts or Brazil nuts, roughly chopped

Equipment
12-hole bun tin

All You Do Is...

1 Line the bun tin with paper cases. Melt the chocolate in a glass bowl set over a pan of simmering water.

2 Take the bowl off the heat, add the Sultana Bran, golden syrup and nuts, and toss till everything is evenly coated.

3 Divide the mix among the paper cases in the bun tin and leave to set in the fridge for about 1 hour.

Storage stuff
Make these the day before and store in an airtight container in the fridge.

Chocolate & Raspberry Cornershop Cookies

These biscuits are great for when you fancy baking on the spur of the moment or with the kids on a rainy afternoon. Pop to the cornershop for what you need.

Makes
25–30
Prep time
20 minutes
Cook time
20 minutes

All You Need Is...

100g dark chocolate
200g butter, softened
100g caster sugar
1 tsp vanilla extract

250g plain flour
1 tsp baking powder
100g raspberry jam
150g fresh raspberries

All You Do Is...

1 Preheat the oven to 160°C (fan), 180°C, gas mark 4. Line two baking trays with baking paper.

2 Melt the chocolate in a glass bowl set over a pan of simmering water, then set aside.

3 Using a hand-held electric whisk or mixer, cream the butter and sugar in a large bowl together till fluffy, then whizz in the vanilla. Mix the flour and baking powder together in a separate bowl, then fold into the butter mixture.

4 Fold in the melted chocolate a couple of times so it looks marbled.

5 Using your hands, roll the mix into conker-sized balls and pop on the baking trays leaving a space around each ball.

6 Put a good thumb print in them and fill the dip with about ¼ teaspoon of jam. Bake for 20 minutes. Take out of the oven and immediately pop a fresh raspberry on top of each one. Leave on the trays till completely cooled.

Storage stuff

These last longer without the fresh raspberry on top so I often make half with raspberries and half without, adding the remaining raspberries before eating.

Hand-me-down
Carrot Cake

For 8

Prep time
15 minutes

Cook time
60 minutes

Freezable
(without
topping)

Handed down to me from my stepmum, this is one of the first cakes
I ever mastered because it's just a case of bunging all the ingredients
in a bowl then throwing it in the oven. The results to this day are a moist
minor miracle that I still can't believe is so easy and *soooo* good.

All You Need Is...

50g walnuts
180g golden caster sugar
150g plain flour
1 tsp ground cinnamon
2 large free-range eggs
2 large carrots, peeled and
    coarsely grated
1 tsp baking powder
100ml olive oil

Topping
200g soft cream cheese
100g icing sugar
finely grated zest of
    1 unwaxed lemon

Equipment
450g loaf tin

All You Do Is...

1 Preheat the oven to 180°C (fan), 200°C, gas mark 6. Line the loaf tin with
  baking parchment.

2 Break up the walnuts a little and mix all the cake ingredients together
  in a large bowl with a spoon. Plop into the tin and bake for 50–60 minutes
  till golden.

3 Leave to cool in the tin while you mix the cream cheese, icing sugar and
  lemon zest together for the topping.

4 When the cake is completely cold, top it with the creamy icing.

Storage stuff
Keep in the fridge – it's even better the next day.

Kids stuff
Don't tell them it's carrot cake unless you want it all for yourself.

END CORNER
MONDAY TU
ESDAY THU
AY WEEKEN

SIDES

Minty Baby Broad Beans

The time it takes to pod these little gems often puts me off using them, as they hide their treasure inside a rather tough little shell. So after a fabulous lunch in my local Greek restaurant, I asked how they got theirs so tender without podding. 'Boil them to hell, lady.' I did, and this great side dish is the rather surprising result – wonderful with lamb, chicken or with a couple of other salads and hummus.

For 6–8
Prep time
5 minutes
Cook time
30 minutes

All You Need Is...

1 x 750g bag frozen baby
   broad beans
2 tbsp extra virgin olive oil

1½ tbsp sherry vinegar
1 heaped tbsp dried mint

All You Do Is...

1 Cover the beans with water (don't include any salt), then bring to the boil and pop on a lid. Turn down the heat and simmer for 30 minutes.

2 Drain the beans, rinse in cold water and dress with the oil, vinegar and mint. Season and serve at room temperature.

Time tip
As a salad this can be made the day before, just give it a stir and serve.

Rosemary Polenta Roasties

For 4–6
Prep time
5 minutes
Cook time
70 minutes

Roast potatoes are always on my menu but this is a great way to bring something new to the table. Served with all manner of Sunday roasts from fish to fowl, these golden spuds are light and crunchy with an Italian twist on a British classic.

All You Need Is...

1kg potatoes, peeled and cut
    into walnut-sized pieces
2 tbsp vegetable oil

4 tbsp dried polenta
handful of fresh rosemary
    leaves, roughly chopped

All You Do Is...

1 Preheat the oven to 180°C (fan), 200°C, gas mark 6. Place the spuds in cold water, bring to the boil, turn down the heat and simmer for 10 minutes. Drain and let them dry in a colander then pop back in the saucepan, pour in the oil and bash about with the lid on till fluffy.

2 Toss in the polenta and rosemary. Throw into a roasting tray and bake for 1 hour till crispy.

Time tip
Parboil, fluff up and coat an hour or two before roasting.

Whizz-up Walnut Pesto

Makes 350g
Prep time
10 minutes

My kids are obsessed with pesto and, as it's so quick and versatile, so am I. This one holds its colour better than a basil pesto and has a wonderful earthy taste that makes me feel all 'Italian peasanty'. Use it stirred through pasta, rice, roasted veg, on bruschetta, fish, chicken or lamb. Because it's homemade it's posh, so don't be afraid to show it off or just use every day in every way.

All You Need Is...

1 x 100g bag watercress
20g fresh mint leaves
2 garlic cloves, peeled
75g walnuts

50g Parmesan cheese,
 finely grated
170ml olive oil

All You Do Is...

1 Whizz everything except the oil in a food processor till very finely chopped then pour in the oil, whizzing to combine. Serve on pasta with garden peas and a handful of baby spinach leaves mixed through.

Time tip

Make double and store in the fridge as the possibilities for pesto are endless.

Little Italian Roasties

Truth is, I eat most of these before they even reach the table. A couple popped in the mouth straight from the oven tray don't count, surely? Three more go missing while scraping them into a serving dish, then six or seven can disappear on route to the table where I announce, 'I'm watching my weight and will only have a few roasties just to join in.' Solution? Make double.

All You Need Is...

800g potatoes, skins on
1 x 80g pack cubed pancetta
1 large red onion, peeled
   and finely chopped

2 tsp dried thyme
1 tbsp olive oil

All You Do Is...

1 Preheat the oven to 180°C (fan), 200°C, gas mark 6.

2 Chop the spuds into very small 1cm cubes. Throw them into a large roasting tin with the pancetta, onion and thyme, then toss in the oil and roast for 35–40 minutes. Give it all a stir halfway through, if you remember. Serve with everything scraped from the base of the tin.

Lemon & Mint Couscous

This is my secret lifesaver. I always keep couscous in the cupboard because there aren't many things you can knock up in a couple of minutes that go so well, with so much. I have a blue cardie that I feel the same about...

For 4–6
Prep time
5 minutes
Cook time
5 minutes

All You Need Is...

350g couscous
4 tbsp olive oil
1 big bunch of fresh mint,
  finely chopped

finely grated zest and juice
  of 1 unwaxed lemon

All You Do Is...

1 Put the couscous in a bowl and cover with 500ml boiling water. Pop a tea towel tightly over the bowl and leave for 5 minutes, then fluff up with a fork.

2 Add the oil, mint, lemon zest and juice.

Storage stuff
Keeps brilliantly covered in the fridge but may need a little more dressing just before serving.

Egg-fried Rice

This is fast food. Simple, nutritious and it goes with a whole load of stuff in my books and a whole load of stuff in everyone else's books; mega useful.

For 3

Prep time
5 minutes

Cook time
10 minutes
(plus standing)

All You Need Is...

200g white basmati rice, rinsed
1 tbsp groundnut oil or olive oil
2 large free-range eggs, beaten

100g frozen peas or petits pois
1 tbsp light soy sauce
1 tbsp toasted sesame oil

All You Do Is...

1 To cook perfect rice every time, pop the rice in a medium saucepan with enough water to cover up to the first joint on your thumb, about 2.5cm above the rice. Bring to the boil, cover with foil, then turn down the heat and simmer for 5 minutes. Turn off the heat and leave well alone for 10 minutes.

2 In a wok or frying pan, heat the groundnut or olive oil then add the eggs and let them start to cook and come together, then stir to roughly break up. Pop in the peas for a couple of minutes. Next, add the cooked rice and stir for 3-4 minutes to bring together, then add the soy and sesame oil to flavour.

Crunchy Coleslaw

For 6–8
Prep time
15 minutes
Cook time
5 minutes

Shop-bought coleslaw just isn't clever. God knows I love a shortcut but not that one. This light, fresh salad is loved by all because it's not drowning in dressing and I have replaced the raw onions with chives which means you can you have a snog straight after. Think barbies, think picnics, think cold meats, think burgers, think jacket potatoes; just don't think twice about making it.

All You Need Is...

100g pine nuts
½ white cabbage, shredded
3 large carrots, peeled
   and grated
80g sultanas
handful of fresh chives,
   chopped

Dressing
2 heaped tbsp garlic mayo
1 tsp Dijon mustard
1 tbsp white wine vinegar
2 tbsp olive oil

All You Do Is...

1 In a dry non-stick frying pan, toast the pine nuts till just golden then add to all the salad stuff.

2 Whisk all the dressing ingredients together and toss with the salad.

Time tip
It's great the next day if kept in the fridge.

Brilliant Brussels with Lemon & Almonds

For years I thought Brussels sprouts tasted of farts, but every Xmas my mum would stamp her feet and insist they were on our festive menu. I would boil the hell out of them, try one, spit it out and prove my point. Then one year I decided to give these little cabbages a chance and I prepared them with love, resulting in a complete turnaround – they are nutty, sweet and full of flavour. The kids love them prepared this way and my mum is looking pretty smug.

For 4
Prep time
5 minutes
Cook time
15 minutes

All You Need Is...

60g whole blanched
  almonds
1 tbsp olive oil

250g Brussels sprouts,
  cut in half
1 unwaxed lemon

All You Do Is...

1 In a non-stick frying pan, dry-fry the almonds till they just start to turn golden, about 3–4 minutes (don't forget them).

2 Add the oil to the pan with the Brussels sprouts halves and fry for about 10 minutes till the Brussels sprouts start to go golden but still have a good bite. Finely grate over the lemon zest, then season, toss and serve not just at Xmas.

Spicy Moroccan Couscous

(To Serve with Just About Everything)

For 4–6
Prep time
15 minutes
Cook time
15 minutes

I love this with lamb, chicken or fish; I love it with other salads; I love it because it will keep so well in the fridge; I love it with flaked smoked mackerel; I love it and I believe...it loves me.

All You Need Is...

2 large onions, peeled
    and thinly sliced
2 tbsp sunflower oil
handful of sultanas
1 tsp mixed spice
1 tsp ground cumin
1 tsp ground ginger

250g couscous
1 x 400g tin Puy lentils,
    drained or 250g pack
    ready-to-eat Puy lentils
juice of ½ orange
1 tbsp olive oil

All You Do Is...

1 Fry the onions in the sunflower oil over a fairly high heat till brown and caramelised, about 15 minutes. Throw in the sultanas and stir for a minute. Now drain them on a piece of kitchen paper.

2 Meanwhile, just mix the three spices with 350ml boiling water and pour over the couscous in a bowl. Cover tightly for 5 minutes then fluff up with a fork.

3 Stir in the lentils and onions and dress with the orange juice and the olive oil. Season and serve.

Storage stuff
This keeps really well if covered in the fridge.

Herby Summer Rice

I love one-pot cooking and this rice dish can be married with almost any recipe in the book. Once you get the hang of cooking rice this way you'll never look back. Feel free to change the courgettes for other favourite green veg – broccoli or peas would also be great; use up those leftover bits and bobs in the veg drawer.

For 4
Prep time
5 minutes
Cook time
15 minutes
(plus standing)

All You Need Is...

½ onion, peeled and
   finely chopped
3 tbsp olive oil
180g basmati rice, rinsed
2 courgettes, trimmed
   and thinly sliced

30g fresh mint leaves,
   chopped
15g fresh dill, chopped
juice of 1 lemon

All You Do Is...

1 In a large saucepan, cook the onion in 1 tablespoon of the oil till just soft.

2 Pop the rice on top and pour in enough water to cover up to the first joint on your thumb (about 2.5cm of water above the rice).

3 Bring to the boil, then immediately lay the courgettes gently on top and cover tightly with foil. Cook over a medium heat for 5 minutes then take off the heat and leave it alone, still covered, for a further 10 minutes.

4 When you are ready to serve just uncover and mix together with the chopped herbs, lemon juice and the remaining 2 tablespoons of oil.

French Peas

You know what they say, 'a woman who cooks leeks and peas in the same pot is unhygienic'. Bad joke, great dish! Serve it with roasts, fish or stews, but frankly I can polish off a whole bowl of this French favourite on its own with just some crusty bread.

All You Need Is...

70g butter
2 leeks, trimmed and finely
  chopped
400g frozen peas
½ iceberg lettuce, roughly
  shredded

80ml vegetable stock
20g fresh flat-leaf parsley,
  chopped

All You Do Is...

1 Melt the butter in a large saucepan over a medium heat. Throw in the leeks and cook for 2-3 minutes. Bung in the peas, lettuce and stock, then pop a lid on tightly and cook for 10 minutes till the leeks are soft and the lettuce is limp. Season and serve with the chopped parsley stirred through.

INDEX

THANK YOUS

I could not have done this without...

Parker and Sonny...you are the best guinea pigs money can buy

Dan...you've worked out how to criticise my food without it landing up in your lap. Respect

Mum and all her Brighton Belles...for continuing to cook up a storm

Lizzy...you've taken me on and made me feel like I deserve to be here

David...your ipod needs some new tunes but your pictures rock

Helen...your charm and patience has been Oscar winning

Martin...that expert northern eye has been invaluable

Bren...you give me the confidence to be confident

Annie and Rachel...the dream team that made the difference

Louisa and Jo...it was a pleasure to watch you in my kitchen

Jo...you can't fault that girl's bowls and jugs

Brigette...for that moist carrot cake and the cooking confidence it gave me

Paul...you've let me stick to my guns and I thank you for it

Charlotte...for kindness, gossip and lashes

Zoe...bless your blowdries and your support in equal measures

Tom Willcocks and the cover day team...that was a laugh

Heike...your enthusiasm knows no bounds

Lucy...you can redesign my life when you've finished the book, please

Kathy...your eagle eye has kept me on track

Gemma...you probably know my recipes better than I do

Everyone in sales and marketing...if it wasn't for you only my Mum and mate Dixie would know about this book

Caroline...you've got me on the sofas and in the mags, now the food's gotta do the talking

Hannah...your backing means I can get baking

All of my pals...keep making my cakes, just stop ringing me from the supermarket

The amazing words of support from those I know and those I don't, to you all...thank you, properly thank you

Fay x

First published in 2012 by Collins
an imprint of HarperCollins*Publishers*
77-85 Fulham Palace Road
London W6 8JB

www.harpercollins.co.uk

16 15 14 13 12
9 8 7 6 5 4 3 2 1

A catalogue record for this book is available from the British Library.

ISBN: 978-0-00-744532-5

Commissioning editor: Lizzy Gray
Project editor: Helen Wedgewood
Food stylists: Annie Rigg and Louisa Carter
Props stylist: Jo Harris
Designer: Lucy Sykes-Thompson

Printed and bound in China by RR Donnelley